Before Truth Set Me Free

Before Truth Set Me Free

Behind the Music to Behind Bars

A Memoir

Vanessa "Fluffy" Murray-Yisrael

MILL CITY PRESS
Minneapolis

Mill City Press, Inc.
212 3rd Avenue North, Suite 290
Minneapolis, MN 55401
612.455.2294
www.millcitypublishing.com

This is a work of nonfiction all the events depicted are true and the characters are real. The events, conversations, and experiences detailed herein have been faithfully rendered as I have remembered them, to the best of my ability. One name has been changed in order to protect the privacy and/or anonymity of the individual involved.

ISBN - 978-1-936400-73-7
LCCN - 2010940712

Printed in the United States of America

To the remnant of Yisrael

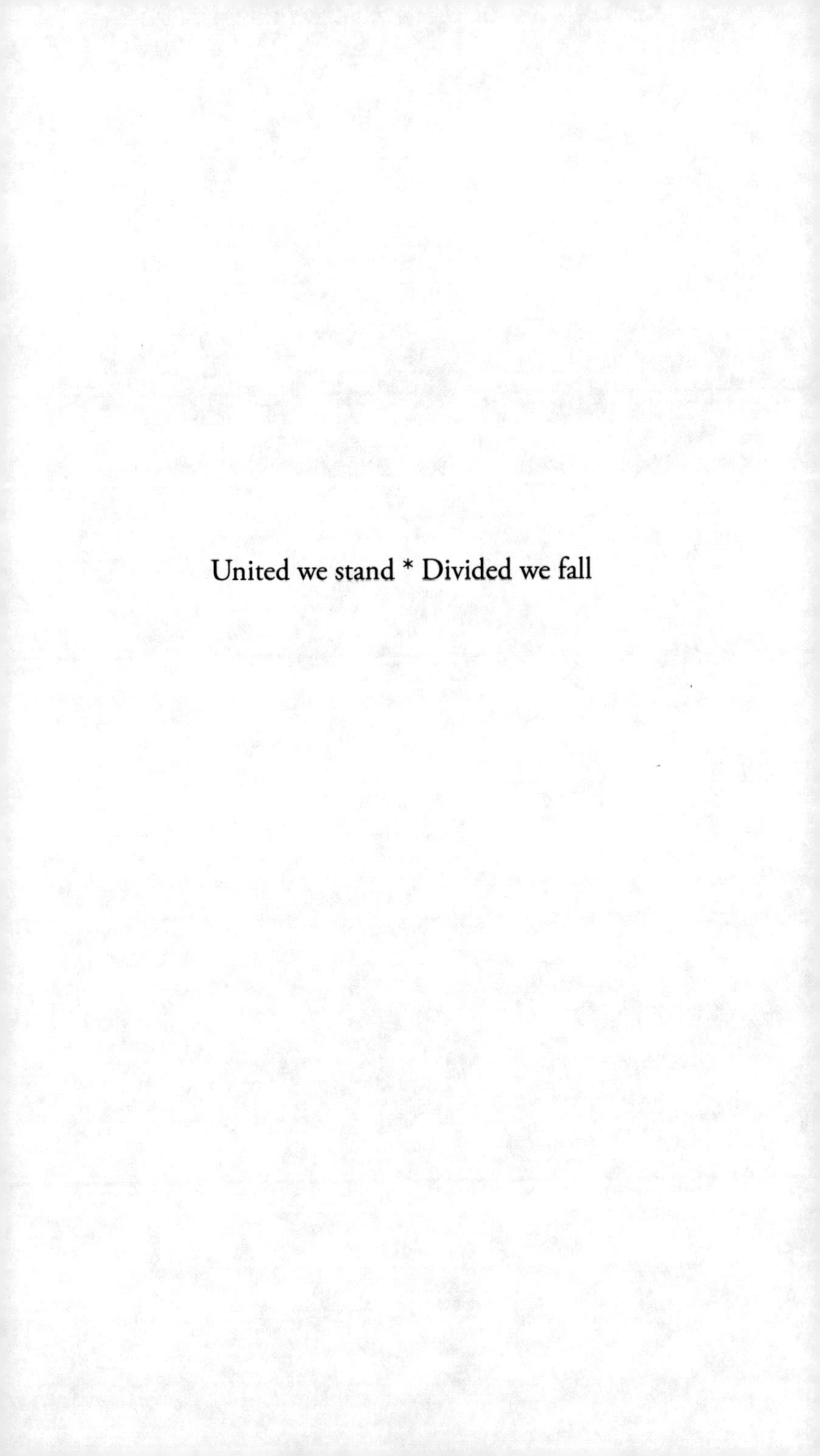

United we stand * Divided we fall

“Life and death, freedom and bondage, hang in the balance of every action we take.”

—Wes Moore

Author of *The Other Wes Moore*

Before Truth Set Me Free

Behind the Music to Behind Bars

A Memoir

Vanessa "Fluffy" Murray-Yisrael

Chapter One

Introduction

Three strikes—you're out! I tell myself as I sit with my bloodstained hands cuffed behind me in the backseat of a police car that's taking me to jail for the third freakin' time. This isn't how my life is supposed to be. I had it all mapped out and going to jail wasn't on my map, wasn't part of my plans. At this juncture I'm supposed to be rich and famous, just like my former colleague, Sean "Puffy" Combs.

You're about to blow uuuuuuup! I tell myself the day I land a gig at Uptown Records. Within less than a year Puffy and I are promoted to top-level executives. As Puffy swiftly climbs the ladder of success, I whoosh down like greased lightning. Where did it all go wrong? Were fame and fortune not my destiny, too?

During the seven-minute ride from San Gabriel Avenue in Decatur, Georgia—the place where I'm arrested—to the county jail on Memorial Drive, I slide my bony wrist out of the handcuffs. When the police car stops at a red light, I contemplate escaping. Conscious that I'll probably not get far before being tackled to the ground and then slapped with another charge—if not shot to death by a trigger-happy cop—I remain seated. Reluctantly I slide the cuffs back on, but this time I keep my hands in front of me.

I spend the rest of the ride thinking about the penalty I'm about to face for my idiotic actions and the negative effect life in prison is going to have on my two children . . . children who'll now have both parents locked up in different states.

My daughter will be fine without me, I reason. She's twenty. My son, on the other hand, just turned seventeen—still a high-schooler and a momma's boy. He is, in a sense, still attached to the umbilical cord. Even though he's visiting his grandmother in New York City for the summer, he desperately needs and depends on me to provide for him, nurture him, and keep him on the right path. Without me around he's sure to go astray. And astray he goes. It isn't long before he quits his summer job at the A&P supermarket to join a gang. It isn't long before he's selling crack. It isn't long before he's sporting a stupid black tear-drop tattoo on his light-skinned baby face next to his left eye. It isn't long before I'm reading about my son in the *New York Post*: "... shot during an apparent drug-related incident on an Inwood street, police said yesterday...when an assailant opened fire on him at 10th Avenue and West 201st Street. The shooter fled…." My son is taken to Harlem Hospital.

The arresting officer turns me over to blue-eyed, middle-aged Detective Buice. He tightens my cuffs as soon as he notices they're loose on my wrists. He places me in the back of his unmarked car. I try to get the cuffs off, but they're now too tight. Oh well, at least my hands are still cuffed in front.

"Am I gon'na get a lot of time?" I ask Buice.

"Yes."

"How much?"

"You're looking at…well, now, let's see…the victim lost a lot of blood…you could be facing twenty years, but…"

Whatever else Buice says, I don't hear him. I'm too busy noticing that smirk on his pale face. Does he think my going to jail is a joke? I'm not going to say anything else to him. It's apparent he's no fan of mine, which is understandable. Nevertheless, those little smirks, super-glued to his face, the ones I keep seeing in the rear-view mirror, piss me off. He reminds me of one of those sleazy detectives in movies. You know the kind—a rogue detective like Alonzo Harris in *Training Day*, the lead character played by Denzel Washington.

We finally reach our destination. Buice gets out the driver's side and walks around. He opens my door and I step onto the curb. I don't know where I am exactly, or what's about to go down. All I know, at this point, is I'm in big trouble. We walk inside one of the many buildings surrounding the jailhouse. Seems like some type of office building. Inside are people, employees or maybe other detectives, sitting at their desks paying us no mind as Buice escorts me through the office. We pass a bathroom. "Can I wash my hands, please?" I ask. We make an about face. I enter the tiny one-man bathroom first, Buice close behind, still smirking. With the door wide open, Buice turns on the water for me, a little cold mixed with a little hot, and stands right behind me while I'm at the sink. I catch a glimpse of myself in the mirror. Whoa! I look like a hot mess. For a quick second I think I'm looking at a crackhead. I'm wearing a tight-fitting, short-sleeve brown t-shirt, gray shorts (which I occasionally wear lounging around the house), and some cheesy white rundown sneakers all splattered with blood. As a matter of fact, blood is splattered everywhere, including the Afro I'm sporting.

It's only been a year since I first decided to embrace my natural kinky curls. I've come to realize that those daggone perms I'd been getting since the age of six did nothing but damage the hair that the Creator of the Heavens and Earth gave me—curly hair that I'm finally learning to accept as beautiful hair. To my amazement, the matted hair I'm looking at in the mirror is hardly beautiful right now.

In addition to the blood there's dirt. Must've found its way there a couple hours ago during the altercation that somehow had me sprawled out on an asphalted driveway sprinkled with dirt and landed me in the care of Detective

Buice. Now my once beautiful 'fro looks stank.

I proceed to scrub my hands as hard as I can to remove the dried blood. Maybe it's just me, but this blood isn't coming off easily. Specks of it are on the upper parts of my arms, too, but I can't reach way up there with these stupid cuffs on.

"Okay, let's go," Buice says after what seems like two seconds.

"I'm not finish," I mutter. "Can't you see I still have blood on my hands? Dang!"

"Excuse me, did you say something?"

"No, just talking to myself."

Buice couldn't care less about me getting cleaned up. In his mind I'm just another stone cold criminal, which is probably the reason he doesn't even bother to give me a paper towel to dry my hands. Oh well, I'll just let them drip dry.

We continue on our journey. Where we're heading, I have no clue. We stop in front of a closed door. He opens it and allows me to enter first. Even though I've never been in this room before, it looks familiar. Just like one of those rooms I've seen on television where those sleazy detectives throw the bad guys so they can give them the third degree or trick them into spilling the beans. The interrogation room! That's what it is.

The room is small and drab. There's nothing in it but a small table, two chairs, and a slab of dirty carpet on the floor. The window, or two-way mirror, is pretty large, and I can see nothing except my reflection when I look in it. Even when

I zero in on it, still nothing. I assume, just as on television, somebody's watching me from the other side.

Inside the lonely room I guess Buice to be about six feet tall, towering over my five-foot-two-inch pocketsize frame. His hair is blonde with a dash of salt and pepper, cropped short, with a gradually receding hairline. If only he'd wipe that annoying smirk off his face for one cotton pickin' minute, he isn't bad looking. The smirk makes him look devilish. He seems fit. No beer belly protruding. He could actually be a ladies' man. Not my type, though. He tells me to stretch out my arms and then inserts a key in my handcuffs, jabbing it in and out of the keyhole numerous times. "I can't unlock the cuffs," he claims, still wearing the smirk. "I'll have to get another key." I don't believe him. He leaves me cuffed in the interrogation room for what feels like hours. In his absence I lay on the stained, carpeted floor in a fetal position, alone, scared, and feeling like a loser in my grubby, blood-spattered clothes. I close my big brown eyes and think about my life.

What in the world am I doing here? Something mighty fishy is definitely going on. Something in the spiritual realm, I'm sure. *Please, God. Forgive me for all my sins; deliver me from evil; show me the true meaning of life. I'm tire, God. I'm tire of running on this treadmill, chasing after the wind. And God, please get me outta here! Pleeeeassseee!*

Detective Buice's entry startles me back to the moment at hand. I uncurl my body and stand. He holds no key and tells me to have a seat in one of the chairs. He sits in the other, the chair facing the two-way mirror, and begins. Since committing felonies isn't exactly my forte, naively I tell him snippets of my version of what happened. I even let him feed me details of what he believes happened, as well.

"You started it, right?" he asks.

"No."

"You swung first, right?"

"Yes...I mean no…I don't know."

"The victim didn't have a weapon, right? You were the only one with a weapon, right?"

"Yes…no…huh?"

Without reading it I sign the confession statement he writes on a pad of lined paper with a pencil, a statement that will probably be used as evidence to assist the prosecution. I don't realize that I have the right to remain silent, even though I've heard it many times on television, and even though the arresting officer robotically recites that speech to me. "You have the right to remain silent. If you choose to give up your right to remain silent, anything you say can and will be used against you in a court of law…."

After Buice is through tricking me, we return to his unmarked car and he drives me to Dekalb County Jail. He turns me over to an African-American female correctional officer. But before he leaves he miraculously unlocks my cuffs without difficulty. "Things that make you go hummmmm," as Arsenio Hall used to say.

After I am fingerprinted, photographed, and processed, the correctional officer ushers me to a small ice-cold holding cell and hands me a plastic bag full of food, even though I have no appetite.

"May I get a blanket, please?" I ask. "I'm freezing in here."

"Don't have any."

Inside the icebox are three other female detainees. By the looks of two of them, I assume they're crackheads. Then again, they probably assume the same thing about me.

"Hey, girl. What's yo' name?" asks one of the crackheads.

"Vanessa."

"Vanessa, do you want your food?" asks the other crackhead.

"No."

"Can I have it?" they ask simultaneously.

"Here."

I reach out to pass a cold bologna sandwich, a moldy orange, and a four-ounce container of milk, which is spoiled, according to the date on the carton. Both crackheads grab at my bag, knocking all the items to the dirty concrete floor. Then both scramble to pick up the nasty-looking food.

"I asked first," says crackhead number one.

"I did!" screams crackhead number two.

"Just look at 'em," whispers the third detainee. "Dem crack ho bitches look like two starved scavengers."

After spending several hours freezing my buns off, the

correctional officer opens the cell door and takes me to a doorless cubicle, where she gives me an oversized, wrinkled orange jumpsuit. The officer holds up a white sheet while I stand inside the cubicle and change out of my blood-spattered clothes. I hand her my clothes and she throws them in a plastic bag. I'm placed in cuffs once again and escorted into an elevator by a half-pint Puerto Rican female correctional officer.

"I heard choo be taking off yo' handcuffs," she says to me in a Spanish-ghetto drawl. She stands several inches shorter than I do and looks to be in her mid to late twenties. I don't respond. She presses the number four button. The elevator moves upward, in slow motion. Terror begins to seep through my body. I imagine being locked up in a tiny cell with a big ol' burly dyke. We finally arrive on the fourth floor, the northeast side of the county jail. There are six dorms—100 through 600—called pods. We stop in front of pod 300. "Oooh, girl. Choo going into cell 301 with that crazy girl. I feel sorry for choo."

A crazy girl? Oh no! Please don't let her be the big burly dyke. I tremble. Thoughts of what will happen to me while locked in a room with a psychotic dyke run through my mind. I mean, after all, I'm not some hooligan. Sure, I've lived in and around tough ghetto neighborhoods and whatnot, but that doesn't make me rough and tough. I see myself as nothing less than a dainty lady.

"Excuse me, Senorita," I beg. "I don't wanna be in a cell

with a crazy girl. Can you please put me in another cell? Pleeeaaassse?"

"Nope. Choo no have no choice here, honey. Choo just do whatever we tell choo. Besides, choo must be crazy, too. I heard what choo did."

The correctional officer sitting in the control booth pops open the metal door to pod 300. Inmates are sitting all around, some rough looking, some ghastly. Some are playing cards, others are sitting in front of a colored television mounted on the wall, and some are in their cells either asleep or standing by their cell door. I feel all eyes trail me as Miss Half Pint escorts me to my new home, cell 301.

Part I

Back in the Day

Chapter Two

The year I was born, Marilyn Monroe was found dead in her Los Angeles home from an overdose of barbiturates. Some say she committed suicide. Others say she was murdered in an attempt to prevent a scandal from toppling the presidency of John F. Kennedy.

That same day, in South Africa, Nelson Mandela began serving twenty-seven years in prison for inciting people to strike, for leaving the country without valid travel documents, and for spearheading the struggle against apartheid.

Two months later Johnny Carson began his thirty-year stint as host of *The Tonight Show*, while James Meredith became the first black student allowed to attend the University of Mississippi. His admission was opposed by state officials and students, sparking a riot that left two dead, more than twenty-five marshals shot, and around one hundred sixty injured.

The so-called blacks were still an oppressed people, long after they had been removed from their land and packed like cargo on ships, lying in each other's feces, urine, and blood. They were scattered across the earth (some ending up in America); suffered at the hands of their enemies; were robbed and stripped of their culture, history, language, and name; then programmed, mis-educated, hoodwinked, bamboozled, and forced to accept their captors' way of life. No longer identified as the nation of Yisrael, they were called Negroes, Niggers, Coons, Jigaboos, Porch Monkeys, Coloreds, Blacks, and years later, African-Americans. They had no recollection of their past, so when their true identity was revealed to them by enlightened ones, they refused to accept it. "Hebrew? Yisraelites? The children of Yisrael? Nah, nigga, dat ain't us!" they said. "Massa say we is Niggers; no, wait, we is African-Americans now." When those in the know told them that land was promised to them, land that stretches from the river of Egypt to the great river Euphrates, they refused to accept it. Instead, they accepted the lie that declared they were going to get forty acres and a mule. "We is staking off land, massa. The Yankees say half belong to us."

By the time I was brought forth, all types of lies and false doctrines were waiting to be dumped on me, too.

Chapter Three

Moms was hit with labor pains during the season that plants bring forth leaves and flowers. She was at Manhattanville Housing Projects on 133rd Street and Broadway, chilling at one of her sister's cribs. She immediately rode the elevator down from the seventh floor to the lobby of building ninety-five. She rushed outside, through the back way of the building, and flagged down a taxi. "Take me to Metropolitan Hospital," she told the cabby. "Hurry. I'm about to have a baby."

Metropolitan Hospital was situated between 97th and 99th Street and First Avenue. That was over thirty-five blocks away from where my moms—whom everybody calls Millie—first entered the taxi. Could she get there in time when her contractions were coming every two to five minutes apart? "My water broke!" Millie yelled out to the cabby. "Hurry!"

The cabby was barely midway to Metropolitan when

my tiny head popped out of twenty-three-year-old Millie's coochie. Millie—even when pregnant was a strikingly rail-thin woman whose dad demanded that she in no way ever cut her long, thick, flowing hair—told the cabby to make a quick detour to the nearest hospital. The cabby swerved around and pulled up in front of Sydenham Hospital in West Harlem. A nurse ran out pushing a wheelchair and helped Millie in. We hadn't even made it inside the hospital when the rest of my five-pound body slid on out. So, technically, half of me was born in a taxicab and the other half on the streets of Harlem. I was pronounced born at eight twenty in the evening on the 21st of May.

Sydenham Hospital mainly served black and underprivileged patients, many uninsured. Even though Millie worked as a teacher's aide at a nursery school in upper Manhattan near Riverside Drive, she wasn't able to make ends meet. For that reason she was on welfare when I arrived, so Medicaid paid my expenses.

Millie named me after the Academy Award-winning British actress Vanessa Redgrave. A few months after my birth, however, Millie started calling me Fluffy. Soon everybody and their momma called me Fluffy. I always kicked the crib blanket with my tiny feet. "That's why I nicknamed you Fluffy," Millie told me. I was her second child.

From the beginning of my days, and long thereafter, I rarely spoke. Instead, I observed everybody and everything. Millie thought I was an extraterrestrial being. "Pssh! Pssh!

Look at her. She's weird," Millie told everyone. I heard that word day in and day out. I didn't know what it meant, but I could sense early on that, in regards to me, it wasn't a very nice word. I could sense early on I wasn't Millie's favorite child.

My brother, Millie's firstborn, came to be one year before me. Millie named him after the romantic swashbuckling actor Tyrone Power. Ty was born at a so-called high-class hospital, a hospital that catered mostly to those of European descent. "Your brother was the only black baby in the nursery," Millie told me later. Ty was supposed to be born at Metropolitan, too, but on his day of delivery Metropolitan was overcrowded. So hospital officials placed Millie in an ambulance and drove her to Flower Hospital on Fifth Avenue and 106th Street.

The Broadway Hotel on 101st Street and Broadway, Manhattan's Upper West Side, became my first new home. We lived there until I was around one, and Millie was in her second trimester of pregnancy. A tiny kitchenette in a hotel was not going to be big enough for Millie's growing family, so she moved us to a small one-bedroom apartment in a five story walk-up tenement on 100th Street and Central Park West.

In 1963, Millie, at last, gave birth at Metropolitan Hospital to her third and final child, my sister, Michelle. I don't know who Millie named Shell after, but whoever she was I'm sure she was white and famous.

My siblings and I have different daddies. Of the three

we met one, my sister's dad, James. For a while Millie told us that James was father to all three of us. He didn't come around much. When he did he paid no attention to any of us little ones. Financially he contributed nothing. His rare visits were mainly an attempt to have sex with Millie. Although I was young, I can still remember the last time he came. It was 1960 something. I lay in bed with Millie and he told her to put me on the couch so he could get in bed with her. "No, you sleep on the couch!" Millie yelled. James sucked his teeth, rolled his eyes, muttered a few unkind words, and stumbled out the apartment with a fifth of vodka in hand.

We saw James a couple more times after that, strolling the streets of Harlem, pushing a handcart full of frankfurters. He'd always give us free franks. And don't nothing taste better than a New York City frank in a bun, smothered with those famous New York City succulent onions. Hmm hmm good! I love New York City franks.

All three dads shirked their responsibility. My dad, perhaps, doesn't even know I exist.

"Your father," Millie told me, "looks like you."

"I guess that means he looks like you, too," I said. Millie and I look very much alike. The only slight differences are hips and buns. Millie has neither.

"Your dad's from Baltimore," Millie told me. "His name is James Shular. He was on break from the navy when I met him. Before he went back to the base, he asked me to marry him."

"So why didn't you marry him?"

"I was confused. Plus, I didn't know I was pregnant when he asked. I told him 'No' and he left and went back to the navy. I never heard from him again."

Why Millie never located my dad so that she could tell him the good news is still suspect to me. *Wasn't I good news?* Even when I tried prying info out of her, she never talked much about any of her baby's daddies, especially my brother's dad. The only thing she said about him was that she'd met him on the day he was released from prison. She's never even told us why he was in prison. Was he a rapist, drug dealer, stickup kid, or murderer? And what was his name? She never told us that either. I wonder if she even knows. Maybe his name is James like the other two.

Our apartment was on the third floor, apartment 3-N. I'll never forget that place. It was the best apartment my family would ever live in, spite of the fact that we had a big hole in the bathroom wall gnawed by rats.

I'll never forget this one beady-eyed rat that held me and Millie hostage in the bedroom. I'd just gotten through taking a bath and Millie was helping me put on my underclothes after getting over the agonizing sting of spraying perfume on my coochie, when all of a sudden we heard a bleat.

"What's that, Millie?"

"A rat is caught in the trap, Fluffy. Let's go see."

We tiptoed to the bathroom, which was connected to the

bedroom, and saw this big, grayish beady-eyed rat squirming, trying to get his head from underneath the medal pedal trap.

"Ahhhhhh! He's getting loose, Millie!" I cringed and jumped behind Millie, who was just as frightened as I was though trying not to show it.

"Ahhhhhhhhhh!" We both screamed as the rat wiggled his head out of the trap.

He was not a happy camper, either. He appeared dazed. His nose was bleeding and he kept flinging his head. Then the conniving little weasel charged us. We ran to the bunk bed and leaped onto the top bunk. Breathless, we sat with our backs against the wall. We waited. No sound. We leaned forward to peek at the floor. "Ahhhhhhhhhh!" That sneaky little rat bastard was right in front of the bed, staring up, mean mugging us with those black beady eyes. He snarled, staring us down from a ready-to-leap stance. We slammed our backs against the wall and waited. No sound. So once again we slowly leaned forward to peer down. He was ambling toward the bathroom. Then he stopped. He turned to give us one last, angry look. If I didn't know better, I'd swear I saw him roll his beady eyes before disappearing into the bathroom.

Millie and I hauled tail from the top bunk, closed the bedroom door behind us, and ran straight to the living room and onto the king-size bed where my brother and sister were sound asleep. There we remained for the rest of the evening.

Other than our neighborhood being multicultural, one of the best things about where we lived was Central Park. We were right across the street. Central Park was the best park in New York City, despite the few times I was flashed a penis. We did everything there: bike riding, swimming, ice skating, roller skating, and sleigh riding. So what if we used cardboard boxes to slide across the snow?

My brother, Ty, was a natural-born daredevil. When the lake froze over in winter, he walked on the ice. One day some thin ice collapsed and he fell into the freezing water. My sister and I didn't know what to do. We watched our dying brother frantically search for the hole he'd gone through. After several attempts he found it and saved himself. I was so relieved! The last thing I wanted to do was run home to tell Millie her beloved son was a goner and that my sister and I had done absolutely nothing but watch him drown.

That near-fatal incident didn't stop Ty from taking risks. He would pretend he was a stuntman or Spiderman and attempt all sorts of life-threatening exploits, including riding on the outside of the IRT train, nearly killing himself once again when he fell and was dragged a hundred feet. These and many other antics gained Millie a headful of gray hair at an early age.

Millie turned half the living room into a second bedroom, which was where we had the king-size bed and two dressers. On the other side were a sofa, two end tables, a coffee table, and an area rug we later discarded because one of Ty's badass friends puked on it and stunk up the whole apartment. On the wall above the sofa was a picture of a white man with long, stringy blond hair and eyes the color of the sea.

"Who dat?" I asked Millie.

"That's the Savior of the world."

"Oh." I didn't consider for one moment that this was the first of many lies and false doctrines that would be dumped on me before Truth set me free.

Millie loved music and she loved to sing. There wasn't a day she didn't have the radio or record player blaring soft rock or Motown. She especially loved Gladys Knight.

Her earliest aspiration was to be a recording artist like her father. "My father and his brothers recorded *Milky White Way*," she told me. I later learned that *Milky White Way* was afterward recorded by Elvis Presley.

My grandfather's singing career was short lived because he decided that drinking alcohol was more important, even though his doctor warned him to stay away from the booze. His liver gave out and when I was still a toddler he died. After that Millie stopped caring for her long, beautiful hair and it withered away.

Unlike me, Millie could carry a tune. In the late 1950s she and two other girls performed in Amateur Night at the Apollo Theatre, Harlem. They escaped getting booed off stage, which meant they were fairly good. After their impressive performance, they found themselves a manager who thought he made it clear when he told them, "As a rule, I don't like managing females because they always seem to ruin things by becoming pregnant. But there's always an exception to the rule."

Millie and her group were on their way to the big time when Millie became pregnant with my brother. That was the end of Millie's dream to be a famous recording artist. But that didn't stop her from singing Gladys Knight and the Pips songs throughout our apartment.

Her love for music was so strong that she rarely missed a concert, especially Gladys Knight. I don't know how she was able to scrape up the extra funds for all the concerts she went to, but she did—and she took me and my siblings along with her.

I don't know about my brother and sister, but I loved the concerts just as much as Millie. The one I remember most was the Jackson Five at Madison Square Garden in downtown Manhattan, on Seventh Avenue between 31st and 33rd Streets. I don't know how Millie pulled it off, but we had great seats, right up front near the stage. Come to think of it, we always had great seats.

I was around nine or ten years old and totally mesmerized by those fine young brothers singing their hit tunes, including *ABC, I Want You Back, The Love You Save, One More Chance,* and *I'll Be There.*

When they sang their last song, they pulled a fast one on the audience. Those little jive turkeys hoodwinked us. The audience didn't know that the show was over and that they'd sung their last song. They pretended they were going to sing another and then whoosh!—they flew off that stage like a rocket, with all the young screaming groupies right behind them. Even security couldn't tame those wild girls. They jumped onto the stage, bogarted their way past security, and chased the Jacksons backstage. I don't know how far those girls got, or if any of them actually caught their prey, but I understood why the Jacksons had to trick us. Those girls were crazy!

At that concert I fell in love with Michael Jackson. But my love for him wasn't quite as strong as it was for Diana Ross. In my eyes no woman on earth was prettier. Okay, there was one other: Marie Osmond of the 1970's *Donnie and Marie Show*. But my focus right then was Miss Ross.

For a long time Miss Ross was all I wanted to be. I wanted to look like her, dress like her, and sing like her, even though I was tone deaf. Nothing else mattered. I went through that period desperately wanting to be this amazingly famous singer whose melodic voice—the one I didn't have—gave listeners goose bumps the way Diana Ross gave them to me. I stood in front of a mirror with a hairbrush in my right hand, imagining it was my microphone. I wore a long, black, silky straight European wig that I had begged Millie to buy me. As I got older I put on tight-fitting clothes and high-heel pumps. I caked my face with make-up. You couldn't tell me I wasn't Miss Ross as I belted out, off key, my favorite

Diana Ross and the Supremes' songs—*Stop in the Name of Love*, *Where Did Our Love Go?*, *Love Child*, and many more. I would later attempt to sing *Stop in the Name of Love* in a beauty pageant and was laughed off stage, but that's a whole 'nother story.

After my looking-glass performances I practiced my acceptance speech for all the Grammy, Billboard, and American Music awards I would surely win someday.

"I want to thank God for giving me my heart's desire. I want to thank all my wonderful fans who love and support me. Last, but certainly not least, I want to give a shout out to all the men around the world that wants me.... Call me!"

Today my acceptance speech would go something like this: "Hear, O Yisrael, you have been chosen to be a set-apart nation, preserved for a specific use. Be stubborn and rebellious no more. Have you not suffered long enough? Why do you think your Abba has scattered you, sending you back to the house of bondage? Just like your ancestors, you've worshipped and given glory to any and every thing except YHWH, He that gives life. Leave those other gods alone and return unto YHWH, O you dry bones. Rise up out of the congregation of the dead. Hear and obey the Word of YHWH. Selah!"

Chapter Four

The year was 1978. I was sixteen and four months pregnant. It was during the era when teenage pregnancy was a pariah. "We think it would be best if you went to a school for pregnant girls," officials at the Louis D. Brandeis High School on West 84th Street told me.

I was supposed to be in the eleventh grade but got held back because the previous year I'd played hooky nearly the whole school term. High school sucked. None of my home girls from around the way were students at Brandeis. And I didn't make any new friends. There was nothing fun to look forward to. I never wanted to attend that school in the first place. I wanted to go to Norman Thomas High School, where students learned shorthand and typing, but I wasn't accepted because my grades weren't up to par. If I couldn't attend Norman Thomas, then staying home (while Millie was at work) watching *Father Knows Best*, *The Brady Bunch*, and *The Flintstones*, was my second choice.

By this time my family and I were no longer living across the street from Central Park. When I was fifteen we moved farther uptown, to Washington Heights, on 164th Street between St. Nicholas and Amsterdam Avenues. This was our third apartment since the day I was born, not including the Broadway Hotel.

The apartment before this one was another five-story walk-up tenement on 129th Street and Amsterdam Avenue, right across the street from Junior High School 43 and Manhattanville Housing Projects, where my mom's favorite sister lived. The apartment was made like a train. All the cars (I mean rooms) were connected in a line. I was eleven when we moved there.

One Hundred Sixty-Fourth Street was by far the worst neighborhood. It was always noisy and heavily plagued by all types of drugs, drug dealers, number runners, and gun shots. It seemed like every morning there was news that another soul was found shot or stabbed to death.

The apartment was in a five-story rodent-infested walk-up. The mice in our apartment were intolerable. They were everywhere, a whole colony of them. They crawled in my bed, up under my covers, and one of them even had the audacity to nibble on my big toe. Ben took the cake though. I spotted him in our kitchen one day. At first I thought he was a big black cat that somehow wormed his way inside our apartment via a window left ajar. He had his back toward me as he ambled toward the stove. I stood at the kitchen doorway pondering how this cat got in. And then I noticed his tail, long and hairless.

Ohmygod! I silently screamed. *That ain't no freakin' cat, that's a Ratzilla!* It looked like a Nutria or an affiliate of the Gambian giant pouch rat family. It was humongous. I'd never seen a rat that size and I pray I never will again.

My baby's father (my baby daddy) was a low-rolling drug dealer and addict. We met roughly five months after my family got settled into our rat-ridden apartment. He was my first sexual encounter. I conceived the first or second time I let him hit it. I was fifteen, soon to be sixteen, and he was eighteen.

"Once you have the baby," school officials said, "you can return to Brandeis."

I was compelled to go to a school for pregnant girls located on East 128th Street in Harlem. There were hardly any students—twenty or fewer pregnant girls. We were all forced to leave our mainstream schools because officials believed it was disgraceful for teens to be walking around a normal school pregnant.

On February 3, 1979, at the age of sixteen, I gave natural birth to a beautiful five-pound girl at Columbia Presbyterian, a hospital four blocks away from where I lived. It was the same hospital that pronounced civil rights leader, Malcolm X, dead on arrival.

My baby daddy tried to assist in the delivery, but he nearly fainted at the sight of all that blood and guck that flowed out of my coochie along with our baby. He was escorted out of the delivery room until he pulled himself together.

He was so excited to be a father for the first time, even though he really wanted a boy. "My baby ain't gon'na want for nothing," he told me.

A few days after giving birth, I went back to Columbia Presbyterian to get myself on birth control pills. I was not going to get myself knocked up again. No siree! The pain of giving birth was too excruciating. OMG! It was the worst kind of pain.

I also went right back to school. I decided to finish out the remainder of the school term at the teen pregnancy school where I was allowed to bring my new baby and then after the summer break I planned to return to Brandeis.

By the time my daughter was five months old, I was pregnant again. Me and those birth control pills didn't quite click. I hated popping them every day, so I didn't. But I certainly didn't want to be pregnant while juggling an infant all at the tender age of seventeen. I decided to get an abortion. If I knew then what I know now, I'd never have done it. Abortion is murder!

After summer break I didn't go back to Louis D. Brandeis, except to tell school officials, "I'm dropping out!" Now that I was a mother, I didn't want to spend another two years in high school. I wanted a job, because the check I was getting from welfare was hardly enough for the things I wanted.

Before Millie eventually quit working and took over as my permanent in-home babysitter, I initially got a free babysitter through some type of voucher program for low-income families. Then I found employment as a cashier at McDonald's on 34th Street. I hated that job, and it obviously showed.

"You're fired!" my supervisor told me after I'd worked there two whole months.

"Why?"

"I don't like your attitude, that's why."

But for a few quick seconds I was hardly sad about losing that smelly job. I thought an office job would be a better fit for me, at least until I was rich and famous. But how in the world was I supposed to work in somebody's office if I couldn't type even ten words a minute? On top of that, I didn't have a high school diploma. It didn't take me long to figure out my next move.

I went to night school and earned my GED. Then I copped a job as a bank teller at the Union Dime Savings Bank in Spanish Harlem. Four months later I was pregnant again. This was my third pregnancy and I was still a teen. No way was I ready to juggle two small children. So once again I made plans to execute another life.

Telling my baby daddy seemed pointless at this point, so I didn't. By this time I was fed up with being his punching bag. Besides that, he never did keep his end of the bargain when he told me, "My baby ain't gon'na want for nothing."

The few times he'd give me money, he'd turned right around, in the wee hours, swearing, kicking, and banging on my front door demanding it back. Millie usually convinced me to give it back to him because he threatened to beat me up if I didn't.

At that time I was pretty gullible, I'd say. I had absolutely no idea that demanding money in the wee hours was one of the signs displayed by drug addicts. How was I supposed to know my baby daddy had an addiction to drugs? He never displayed any recognizable signs. He always wore clean clothes and fresh new kicks. I had no idea he was a stickup kid, too. How was I supposed to know that? He never took me with him on his robbery sprees, nor did he discuss that part of his life with me. It wasn't long before his lifestyle landed him in prison, and that's where he spent the greater part of his life.

I was around ten weeks' pregnant on the day I was scheduled to have abortion number two. Millie tagged along and sat in the waiting room while I was escorted into the operating room. I lay flat on my back, legs propped up, moments away from murdering another fetus, when suddenly a boyish-looking Caucasian nurse walked in. She wasn't the same nurse that had moments ago stepped out of the room and told me she'd be right back to perform the operation. No, she was a different nurse.

"Vanessa," she said. "We're not going to give you an abortion."

"What!" I shrieked as I sat up. "Why not?"

"I'm sorry. We can't do it."

"But why not? I don't want to have this baby."

"Would you like to speak with a therapist?"

"For what? I just want an abortion!"

Moments later I was in another room, smaller than a jail cell, sitting across from a woman with long black hair wearing a white lab coat. *No way is this her office*, I thought. *It's way too tiny*. Inside was a small table with two chairs and no therapist couch. If I didn't know better I'd swear we were sitting inside of what used to be a mop closet.

"Why are you crying?" the therapist asked.

"I want an abortion and the nurse won't give me one. Do you know why?"

I can't remember the entire conversation, but I remember it was as short and empty as the look on her white-skinned face. The therapist acted as eerie as the nurse. And just like the nurse she gave no explanation to my simple question before I stormed out of her office, weeping like a baby, and into the waiting room where Millie sat. Tears streamed down her face, too.

"Why are you crying?" I asked her.

"I don't want you to get an abortion," she confessed for the first time. "Why are you crying?"

"They said they can't give me an abortion." Millie's face lit up as she jumped and clapped for joy. "I don't know why you're so happy. I'm going somewhere else and get it done. I don't want this baby!"

I tried to make sense of that bizarre day. Why was I given no explanation whatsoever? I tried to make sense of Millie's behavior. Why was she so concerned about the life of my third fetus when she hadn't cared that I aborted my second fetus? I tried to make sense of the fact that I never did make an appointment at another abortion clinic. And then when I became pregnant a fourth time—after giving birth to my third fetus, of course—why was I successful at aborting the fourth fetus? Come to think of it, why was I successful at aborting the fetuses before and after the third fetus? Who was this (third) fetus that I couldn't murder? And the nurse who denied my abortion…was she really a nurse or an angel?

On June 27, 1982, I gave birth to a five-pound, two-ounce beautiful pale-skinned baby, the third fetus.

My baby daddy wasn't there during the delivery of our second born. As a matter of fact, my baby daddy and I hadn't spoken to each other for nearly six months prior to the birth of this mysterious child. Even when we'd seen each other in the streets, we'd walked past as if we'd never met. But the day my baby daddy found out I'd given birth to a boy who looked exactly like him, he rushed to the hospital.

"Vanessa, please name him after me," he begged and

pleaded, tears rolling down his face. "Please, baby! Please give him my name!"

Chapter Five

Three months after the birth of my son, who was named after his daddy, I enrolled in Katharine Gibbs, a private business school on Park Avenue and 42nd Street, and earned a certificate in word processing. My new skills led to a State job as an information specialist, a fancy name for word processing operator or typist.

During this time my craving for spiritual food kicked in. I wanted to know the Creator of the Heavens and Earth better. *What does He require of me? What must I do to please Him? What is my purpose?* I sought answers by watching all types of religious programs, reading the Bible, and attending church services regularly. And believing this was the way to receive salvation, I got baptized at the age of twenty-two at a Baptist church on 125th Street in Harlem. Afterward I wanted to talk about nothing but sweet Jesus, a name commonly used in Christianity—a name I called on before Truth set me free from worshipping a hippie on a stick–no offense.

"You're going to turn people off if you keep talking about Jesus," said a ventriloquist interested in dating me.

"You should experience life instead of going to church all the time," one of my aunts told me. "Get out and see the world, date different men, have fun. You're too young for all this churchy stuff."

I never found the answers to my questions at the Baptist church on 125th Street. All I found was a no-sense-making preacher who yelled and screamed and parishioners who fell onto the floor or ran around the church building as if possessed. I got tire of ducking my head down for fear that one of the out-of-control parishioners was going to knock me upside my head.

Before long my craving for show business kicked in harder than ever. I craved the entertainment world as much as the spiritual world. I was drinking out of two cisterns. But, truthfully, the entertainment world had the spiritual world beat by a mile. Make that twenty miles.

It wasn't long before I—like a dumb-dumb—took an unnecessary three month leave of absence (and never returned) from my fairly decent, pretty secure, though a tad boring, job as an information specialist to work temp assignments. It wasn't long before I stopped going to church and placed my Bible back on its shelf to collect dust as I set out to chase after fame, fortune, and, along the way, a big-time rap star.

Part II

Behind the Music

Chapter Six

In my dreams he was my boo, and baby daddy number two. But in reality he was nothing more than a pathway to a gig I had never even considered.

The first time I saw him in person was at the Silver Shadow night club where he was scheduled to perform. It was 1985. I managed to worm my way right up to the front of the stage. I had to get close up on my boo, who was sporting a headful of curls. Thank goodness there wasn't any greasy activator juice dripping from his curls. Yuck!

For three nights in a row, after his dazzling performance at the Shadow, he was all up in my dreams. The dream that stayed in my head the longest was the one where I stood in a silent desert wearing a long, white, flowing gown. He crept up behind me and swirled me around to face him. His touch startled me, but he quickly calmed me down, gently grabbing my face with his two big hands. He slipped his wet tongue in my ear, kissed my neck, and then *wham*! He thrust his tongue down my throat. At first I gagged, but seconds later I moaned and groaned as he tongued me down for what seemed like an hour. After the long, passionate kiss, he undressed me, throwing my gown across the desert, and we made wild, crazy love in the sand. We did every position imaginable—doggy style, missionary, cowgirl, standing, sitting, T-square, sixty-nine, wheelbarrow—until the break of dawn. I was in seventh heaven. On the verge of exploding into an orgasm, I woke up drenched in sweat, disappointed that it was only a cotton-pickin' dream.

He was one of the biggest rap stars of the '80s. He had a unique way of using his mouth to imitate drum machines and samples of oldie-but-goodie tunes. He became known by many as the original human beat box and the greatest entertainer. I was totally in lust with homeboy, and I had to find a way to turn my dreams into reality. I just had to meet him. But how? I couldn't be just another groupie, or at least I couldn't let him know I was precisely that. I had to be much more if I wanted to get his attention. I needed a master plan. So I put on my thinking cap to devise a grand scheme to capture my boo.

I made up my mind to search out jobs that allowed me to meet and mingle with celebrities. I convinced myself that as an industry insider I was certain to bump into my boo.

Full of zeal, I submitted my resume to entertainment firms, and it wasn't long before I received a phone call from Gloria, the managing editor of *Black Teen Magazine*.

"I received your resume, Vanessa. Unfortunately, we do not have any openings here at *Black Teen*. What I would like to offer you is a position with another publication. We're in the process of starting up a new magazine called *What's Hot*, but it will be a few months before that publication is up and running."

"Sounds marvelous! I would love to be a part of *What's Hot*."

My conversation with Gloria was fairly brief. During our pleasant exchange I casually asked why my boo had never been in any issues of *Black Teen Magazine*.

"I've been trying to get an interview with Doug E. Fresh for quite sometime," Gloria replied. "I can't seem to get one."

That was all I needed to hear. "I can get an interview with Doug E. Fresh!" I blurted out.

"Oh, really? And how are you going to do that, Vanessa? If I can't get an interview with him, and I'm the managing editor, how are you going to get one?"

"I can! I just know I can! He's performing at the Red Parrot tomorrow night, and I plan to be there. I'll let you know how the interview turns out."

"I highly doubt you'll get an interview, Vanessa. Like I said, I've been trying to get those folks at Reality Records to set something up, but they never do. I've placed Doug E. Fresh and his management on my shit list."

After we hung up I danced the wop (an '80s craze) all around my bedroom, shouting, "Yes, yes ya'll; to the beat, ya'll; I'm in the house, ya'll; God is good, ya'll!"

My plan to meet Fresh was in full swing.

Chapter Seven

The Red Parrot was a huge, trendy nightclub between 11th and 12th Avenues on 57th Street where big-name artists, such as Madonna, performed.

A neon parrot, ten or eleven feet high, stood in the entrance hall. Real live red tropical parrots lounged the night away in sound-proof glass cages—when partygoers tapped on the glass, the birds couldn't hear.

There were three bars. The main bar, closest to the dance floor, had five to seven bartenders working at the same time. The passageway leading to the dance floor was fenced with chrome wire.

I was a frequent visitor to the Parrot. I knew my way all around that joint. What's more, I'd had the pleasure of performing live on the Parrot's rotating, see-through glass stage the year before Fresh's performance.

I was one of three back-up models for Milk and Gizmo,

a local rap group known as the Audio Two. Most hip hop heads knew them for their hit single *Top Billin*, off their 1990 *What More Can I Say* album.

The Audio Two and their manager-dad spotted me and the other two models, Purple and Peggy, at a beauty pageant rehearsal held at a downtown Manhattan club. Milk and Giz had a few shows lined up and were at the pageant rehearsal scouting out a couple cute girls to prance around them on stages around town to help promote their first 12" single, *A Christmas Rhyme*.

Their dad noticed Purple and Peggy and instantly recruited them. Purple, nineteen, was a striking Puerto Rican with long, black silky hair. She resembled recording artist, Vanity. Peggy, a sensual, dark-skinned sister who sported a long, lustrous weave, later went on to become a video vixen as well as a background singer for Diana Ross. She was about twenty-one.

Nat Robinson, the Audio Two's manager-dad, was especially smitten with Peggy. He was so busy drooling over her he didn't even notice me, a twenty-three-year-old who could pass for seventeen. Fortunately for me, eighteen-year-old Giz noticed me.

Although the gig at the Parrot was our second or third performance with the Audio Two, it was the first big show, a show with major artists on the bill. Me, Purple, and Peggy would be on the same bill, performing to a packed house. I was mad hyped!

I wore the same outfit that I always wore—a leopard dress clinging to the contours of my petite, shapely body. It was split up the side and fell right below my knees. Purple and Peggy wore formfitting outfits, too.

Scheduled to perform that night were female group 9.9, famous for their 1985 hit *All of Me for All of You*. There was also Val Young, famous for looking like a black Marilyn Monroe and for her 1985 album, *Seduction*, which was produced by Rick James. To top it all off, Rick James showed up to support her.

"Can I take a picture with you?" I asked Rick as he and an older woman sat on the staircase leading to the dressing room.

"No," he said. "I'm trying to spend time with my mother right now."

Oh, please! Spare me the baloney! I thought, rolling my eyes as I walked away. Fifteen minutes later I spotted him taking a picture with Peggy. *Oh, snap!* Not only did he take a picture with her, he seemed to drool all over her the same way Nat Robinson did. Later that night Peggy told me not only Rick but also Eddie Murphy had tried to get the hook up and gave her their phone numbers. Guess I didn't have the right look.

Also scheduled to perform that night were rap stars Salt-N-Pepa. They were promoting their first single, *The Show Stoppa*, which dissed Doug E. Fresh's hit single *The Show*.

As is normal in the music biz, we arrived at the Parrot

a few hours before showtime for sound check. Salt-N-Pepa showed up, too. They weren't there long before a big, black grisly-looking man went off on them.

"Get out of here!" grisly man yelled.

"Come on, Sandy," Salt said while walking toward the exit. "Let's just go."

"Nah, this shit ain't right," Pepa said, nearly in tears, while trying to stand her ground. "He can't do us like this. Fuck that!"

Pepa refused to leave. She continued to yell back at the big, beefy man. A puny dude I invited claimed he knew Pepa personally, so he walked over to her. "You need some help?" he asked.

"Nah, I'm all right," Pepa said.

"Get the fuck out of here!" yelled the big man again, walking toward Pepa. I was scared for her. He looked as if he was going to actually pick her up and throw her out.

"This shit ain't right," Pepa yelled, reluctantly storming out of the club in a huff before the beefy man could reach her.

Showtime! As usual the club was full to capacity. The Audio Two were the opening act, and me, Purple, and Peggy joined them on stage. We had no particular routine rehearsed, so the three of us sashayed around Giz and Milk as if we were high fashion models.

"They ain't nobody," I overheard a couple of haters in the

audience say as they watched us strut our stuff.

"Coming to the stage next is Supernature!" the emcee announced. Loud cheering erupted from the audience. But then, lo and behold, two scared-looking tack heads pretending to be Salt-N-Pepa (aka Supernature) stepped on stage right behind the microphones. Of course I wasn't surprised to see a fake Salt-N-Pepa, not after what I witnessed during sound check. The cheering instantly stopped.

"Who the hell are they?" partygoers demanded.

When the fake Salt-N-Pepa opened their mouths to lip sync *The Show Stoppa*, all I heard was "Boooooo! Get your raggedy asses off the stage! Boooooooooooooooo!" And I ain't ashamed to admit I was one of the booers. After all, the real Salt-N-Pepa were my favorite female rappers and there was no way I was going to stand there and let those two tack heads, bless their young hearts, pretend to be Sandra Denton and Cheryl James. No, siree! Those two young girls didn't stand a chance at replacing the real Salt-N-Pepa

What that big beefy man failed to comprehend was that Cheryl and Sandy had generated a lot of fans from that one song in a short period of time, and it was much too late to replace them because everybody knew what they looked like. At least every young hip hop head in New York City did.

The night Doug E. Fresh was scheduled to perform, I arrived at the Parrot extra early to beat the crowd. It was spring 1986. I was aware that security didn't get beefed up until the place was nearly packed—usually around midnight—giving me fewer bouncers to sham while I tried to sneak to the dressing rooms to find my boo. Usually I went to the Parrot with Purple, sometimes with my other home girl, Butter, and sometimes alone. This night was special. I didn't want any distractions, so I went alone. Besides, it was harder to slink around with others tagging behind me.

Wearing a semi-conservative two-piece beige pants outfit, I stood near the stairs leading to the dressing rooms preparing a story to tell the on-duty bouncer, who blocked the stairwell. Lucky for me I didn't have to sham up anything because he suddenly left his post. I dashed up. As I neared the top, I heard lots of people talking and laughing. One of the doors was wide open. Some people were in the room and some stood outside, in front of the door. "Excuse me," I said, pushing my way through. I scanned the small room and found him. He stood in the middle of the room, surrounded by guests. He was tall, dark, slender, and mouthwatering. I strode toward him. He saw me coming and looked me dead in the eyes. My heart skipped a beat, but I managed to remain calm. I stopped right in front of him, head to head. He ignored everyone else and continued staring me down, curious to know who I was and what I wanted. I had his undivided attention as I extended my hand to shake his.

"Hi, Doug E. Fresh. My name's Vanessa. I'm a reporter for *Black Teen Magazine*. Can I interview you?"

"Sure," he said without hesitation. "Let me introduce you

to my road manager and he'll set it up."

He escorted me a few steps to an elderly Latino man with salt and pepper hair. Fresh introduced us and instructed his roadie to set up the interview. Then Fresh shook my hand once again and left me standing there. The road manager gave me a time and place. I thanked him and darted out of the room, bursting with excitement.

Chapter Eight

"I have a doctor's appointment this afternoon," I lied to my supervisor. "Can I take the rest of the day off?"

"No, you can't," he yelled. "If you leave, don't come back!"

It wasn't a difficult choice. Was a measly temp assignment more important than interviewing Mr. Fresh? This was, perhaps, my only chance to meet him, and I wasn't going to let nothing or nobody stop me. I grabbed my purse and jacket and said good-bye to one of my coworkers.

"Vanessa, you're going to lose your job over Doug E. Fresh?" my coworker asked, giving me the you're-so-stupid look.

"I can always get another temp job, but I can't always get the chance to meet Doug E. Fresh."

I walked out. I stopped at an electronics store to purchase a sixty-dollar cassette recorder, then rushed over to 12th Avenue and Fifty-something Street to see my boo.

Fresh was at an indoor video shoot. When I arrived, I rang the doorbell and the roadie opened the door. Instead of a welcoming smile, I got a sort of frown and a lame excuse that was intended to convince me to leave.

"You'll have to wait until the shoot is over before you can interview him. That could be hours."

"I don't mind waiting," I said.

A tad annoyed that I didn't go away, he escorted me to a game room. Inside I met Fresh's little brother and a few of his friends.

"Who are you?" they asked.

"I'm a reporter for *Black Teen Magazine*," I told them as I whipped out my tape recorder. "And who are you?" I asked a young dude lining up balls on a pool table.

"I'm Doug's best friend."

"Is that so? Why don't you come have a seat over here and tell me all about your relationship with Doug E. Fresh."

He was only too happy to oblige, and so was Fresh's little brother, whom I interviewed later. I spent the next couple of hours hanging in the game room, enjoying Fresh's handsome little brother and friends until one of the video girls came into the room. She told me her name was Shana and that she was seventeen. She told me her mother was Susan L. Taylor, the driving force behind *Essence Magazine* and the author of several books. I could see the resemblance.

Shana was wearing a short, black, tight-fitting skirt with a yellow top the length of a mini dress covering the top half of the skirt. She had a big black belt around her waist, and most of her hair was pushed back into a long ponytail, with the exception of a wide bang that reached her eyelashes. She was very cute, just like her mother.

She gave me a look that appeared to say, "I'm hating on you." Then she questioned me about who I was and how old I was and why I was there. Initially, I didn't like sista girl's attitude, and I wondered if she was dating Fresh. After some time had passed, I realized she was a sweetie pie who hardly was hating on me. That was just a figment of my stuck-up imagination.

I was having such a great time that I decided to share some of it with my friends. I called my two Puerto Rican home girls, Purple and Ester, and told them to come on down to the shoot. "Bring a camera with you, Ester," I said before hanging up the phone.

When they arrived we all hugged and kissed and then headed straight to a room where Fresh and his crew were shooting their video for "All The Way to Heaven," one of Fresh's songs off *Oh, My God*, his first album. They were lip syncing and dancing on a stage shaped like a phonograph record. Ester immediately started snapping away like a professional photographer.

During one scene Fresh wore a couple of big gold chains around his neck, white sweat pants, and a red wife beater with the word Bally on the front. Fresh, his crew, and the teeny-bopping video girls swung their heads from side to side, their arms moving in the same direction. I couldn't take my eyes off Fresh. He saw me watching him and waved. I wanted to pass out. Instead, I smiled and waved back.

The shoot finally ended around ten o'clock that night. Fresh and his crew and me and my crew all entered a stairwell that would lead us back to the game room, one flight up. I could hear Fresh's voice right behind me. I turned around to reintroduce myself only to find him looking at my gluteus maximus.

Inside the game room, Fresh and I sat face to face on a sofa. He was sweaty, but he sho'nuff looked good to me. I hoped I looked good to him in my black leather-look four-inch slides, white ankle-length tight cotton skirt with black polka dots that accented my curves, and a black sleeveless mock neck that showed off my toned arms.

While my crew and his crew played pool, I whipped out my cassette player.

"Do you mind if I record you?"

"No, I don't mind."

I pressed record and took out a white five-by-eight pad with a list of questions I'd prepared the night before. *If Fresh sees me with a recorder and a list of questions, he'll no doubt believe I'm the real thing. Isn't that how real reporters do it?*

"Why are you reading your questions?" he asked. "I like reporters that speak straight from the heart."

Fresh was probably unimpressed with my doofy cassette player, too. I should've bought one of those cute little handheld voice recorders, but the doofy player was less expensive. Oh well. Slightly embarrassed by his comment, I ignored his request to put away the list and continued interviewing him.

"So, what type of kid were you?"

"Noisy. I used to stand on the tables in the lunchroom rapping over beats that another kid made banging on the food trays. Some days, me and Barry B and Chill Will cut school and hung out at Barry's house playing music and practicing raps and eating peanut butter and jelly sandwiches."

"How did you get into the music game?"

"At a New Edition concert. The crowd was getting restless waiting for New Edition to perform, so I got on stage and rocked. I had the crowd going wild."

Since my main quest was to become acquainted with Fresh on a sort of intimate level, I needed to find out if he was booed up and whether or not we were compatible.

"Is there a special lady in your life?"

Fresh paused for a split second, showing me a sheepish grin. "The only special lady in my life right now is my mother. I don't have time for a girlfriend right now because I'm on a mission with no luggage. After I finish the mission, then whoever I find that can deal with me, I'll be with that person."

Delighted to hear that my boo didn't have a significant other, I continued. "What qualities do you look for in a girl?"

"Sweet personality and very nice. She must understand me and what I'm doing. At the same time, if she respects me, then I'll respect her in return. I also want someone who wants to have a lot of children because I like children." Fresh interrupted our interview to crack a few jokes on his little brother, who was nearby playing Pac-Man. The brothers went back and forth joning each other. I chuckled at their silly jokes. Before Fresh turned his attention back to me, he yelled one last crack. "You dirt rag!" I laughed out loud and before long Fresh roared with laughter, too.

The interview continued, but this time nineteen-year-old Fresh hurled a few questions at me.

"How old are you?"

"Twenty-four."

"You don't look it. Who did you say you work for?"

"*Black Teen Magazine*."

He gazed into my eyes. And his eyes told me I was busted, that he knew I was really a groupie perpetrating a fraud.

"You're clever," he said, still gazing. I turned my attention back to my pad and hit him with the next question.

"Your latest single, *Nuthin*, is a rap against crack. How do you feel about the drug problem in our society?"

"Crack is simply the devil in another form. Leave crack alone!"

"What is your religious belief?"

"I'm not into any particular religion. I just believe in the Bible, the Old Testament only."

Today his statement, "Old Testament only," makes sense to me. A lot of sense. Then I wondered, *What's wrong with the New Testament?*

"How do you want people to perceive you?"

"I try to write rap songs that have a message because I don't want people to perceive me as being a street kid with no dollars and no sense."

Fresh's roadie walked up and interrupted. "The owner is ready to lock up. Vanessa, if you want you can finish the interview while we're walking out."

I decided to end the interview on the sofa with one last question.

"What are your future goals?"

"To put out the biggest rap record in history, win a Grammy, attend law school, and buy my mother a house in Barbados."

I thanked Fresh for his time. We stood up. He gave me a hug and kissed me on my cheek. I wanted to scream *Hallelujah!* But as a new member of the press I had to remain poised and professional. The groupie scream came out later, when Fresh and his crew were out of sight.

Chapter Nine

I couldn't wait to tell Gloria how easy it was for me to cop an interview with the original human beat boxer. Oooh, I could not wait! I called her the next day.

"Whaaaaaat!?" she shrieked when I told her how it all went down. Gloria was heated. "I can't believe this! I'm going to let Doug E. Fresh and his managers have a piece of my mind. I cannot believe they let you interview him and not me. Oh, hell no! You're not even a real reporter."

"Now I am," I mumbled to myself. After Gloria finished venting, I told her I taped the whole interview. "I'll make a copy and send it to you in the mail."

I took it upon myself to write a story about Fresh, too. It only made sense to me. After all, I was the one who had orchestrated and conducted the interview, so why should someone else write the story?

When Gloria received my package, she called me to say

she was very impressed and that she was going to publish the story I wrote in the next issue of *Black Teen*. I was elated.

"Did you take any pictures, Vanessa?" Gloria asked.

"My friend, Ester, took a whole bunch of pictures, but none of them came out right, so no, I don't have any pictures."

"That's okay. I have a picture of Doug E. Fresh. I'll use that."

Before long *Black Teen* hit the newsstand. Gloria sent me a big glossy tear sheet of my story, a copy of the magazine, and a check for fifty bucks. I was overjoyed for days, even though Gloria botched my story by adding something she had no business adding. Because of that I had to explain the addition to Fresh when I ran into him at a celebrity party I crashed.

"I didn't tell you I was a Jehovah Witness," Fresh said.

"I know. The editor added that to my story without my knowledge. I'm sorry."

In spite of the mix-up, I was grateful to Gloria for publishing my first piece of writing. *I am the real thing now,* I told myself. *A professional writer*. I couldn't believe that my very own story with my very own byline was actually in a magazine that thousands of teenagers read each month. At the bottom of my story were the words "Vanessa Murray is a freelance writer based in New York City. This is her first story for *Black Teen*."

It felt good to see my story and name in print. It made me

feel like some sort of big cheese. I wanted to keep feeling like that. My lust for Fresh didn't make me feel like that, so my craving for him abruptly took a back seat to writing.

When Gloria didn't call me soon enough for a job at *What's Hot Magazine*, I certainly wasn't going to sit around and wait. I was anxious to see my name in print again. So I submitted my resume and my Doug E. Fresh clipping to other publications. I received a call one week later from Rene John Sandy, Publisher of *Class Magazine*. He offered me a position right over the phone, sight unseen. He hired me to be the assistant to the editor, however my job entailed assisting no one. I worked solely on my own as a reporter/writer for the publication. I made appearances at luncheons, parties, and various social gatherings. Sometimes I'd walk up to public figures and interview them right on the spot, but most times their publicists arranged the interviews. One publicist did not appreciate me interviewing his client without his permission. He rolled up on me and his client, actor Carl Payne (Cole of the Martin Lawrence sitcom), one evening while we sat at a two-man table at a New York City club.

"What's going on here?" the publicist demanded.

"She's interviewing me," Carl replied.

"For what? Who are you?" he asked me. "I didn't set this up." I told Carl's angry publicist my name and the name of the magazine I worked for and handed him my cheesy business card. "Before you publish a story on my client, I need to see it first!" he demanded.

I did not appreciate his snotty attitude. I ignored him and turned my attention back to Carl as his angry publicist walked away.

"Showtime!" someone announced over a loud speaker. Carl and I rose up from where we sat and quickly walked over to the front of the stage. We wanted no problems seeing Bobby Brown perform songs from his 1986 debut album, *King of Stage*.

Life at *Class* was short-lived. As it turned out, the company had financial issues. As a result I rarely got paid.

I and a couple of other employees had had enough of Mr. Sandy's lame excuses every pay day, so we called it quits.

Not only was I out of a job, I was also without a place to live. Not including my brother—who was incarcerated and would serve over thirty years in and out (mostly in) of penal institutions—my family and I were evicted from our apartment on 164th Street where we had lived for ten years. We moved in with Millie's favorite sister in the Manhattanville Housing Projects. After a couple of months that situation turned ugly for me, and I alone was told to get out because I refused to pay for collect calls from one of my cousins' incarcerated boyfriend.

With just a shopping cart filled with some of my belongings, I hit the streets. It didn't seem to make sense for my children to roam around homeless, too, so, I decided to let them remain at my aunt's place in Millie's care until I could cop my own apartment. Meanwhile I lived like a gypsy, sleeping at this friend's house and that friend's house, from the Salvation Army to the YWCA. I also went back to temping until the day I came across a tiny ad in a local newspaper: "Receptionist wanted at an entertainment firm."

Chapter Ten

I submitted my resume to an address on Warren Street in Brooklyn. Not long after I received a call from Sandra Zuniga, the company's office manager. A week later, in the autumn of 1988, I was the receptionist at Uptown Records, a relatively new management firm whose roster included recording artists Heavy D, Al B. Sure!, Guy, Groove B Chill, Finesse & Synquis, Father MC, and The Gyrlz, to name a few.

The company was located at the same address where I'd submitted my resume, a two-story condominium. The living room, on the main level, was my domain. Also on that level were the main entrance, a kitchen, small bedroom, and bathroom. Down the spiral stairs were three small bedrooms turned into offices and occupied by executives and their assistants, including CEO Andre Harrell and his pretty assistant, Jill Woodlon.

One of my favorite coworkers spent a lot of time hanging out in the reception area with me. I could never figure out what his job entailed. I didn't even know his job title. All I knew was that he kept me amused . . . except for the one time he stood in the kitchen, straight across from my desk, to show me what he was working with.

"Look, Vanessa," he said.

"Oooooh! I'm telling Andre on you," I shrieked, turning my eyes from him.

"No, Vanessa, please don't tell Andre." He quickly tucked in his big black wee wee.

"I'm telling, you pervert!"

"Vanessa, noooooo, please don't tell. I'm sorry. Please, please don't tell Andre."

"Okay. But you better not do that again, pervert!"

I never told Andre or anyone else. In spite of that offensive occurrence, the brother was a fairly nice guy. I'll never forget the time he took up for me. As was the norm, he invited me to hang out with him after work, no place in particular.

"I need to make a stop at Carl's house," he said.

"Okay," I said.

Carl, a New York City cop by day and a security guard for some of Uptown's parties by night, lived a couple of blocks from the office, so, my coworker and I walked over. Carl invited us in. I made my way to a sofa in the living room while my coworker stood by the front door conversing with Carl. Moments later Carl's roommate, another New York cop, arrived home. When he saw me sitting there, he came and sat beside me. Then he turned and looked at me with a big Kool-Aid smile on his face and all of a sudden leaned toward the floor and began grabbing at my shoes, as if trying to remove them from my feet. "What are you doing?" I tried to push him away. He didn't respond and struggled with me to remove my shoes. "Stop!" I yelled. He paid me no mind. It made no sense.

My coworker, still communicating with Carl on the other side of room, heard my cry and saw what was going down. "Stop it, man!" he demanded. "She's not like that!" At that moment I realized what this cop was actually trying to do to me. *But why the shoes first?* "Come on, Vanessa, let's go," my coworker said. I was happy to comply.

As we walked to the nearest corner to flag down a cab, we made no mention of what had transpired between me and that sleazy cop.

Chapter Eleven

Right around the time I joined the staff at Uptown, or shortly before, Andre Harrell received a large sum of money to merge with MCA Records. Half the staff, including Andre and his assistant, moved to new headquarters on the west side of 57th Street in Manhattan—in the same building and on the same floor as MCA and Motown Records. I remained in Brooklyn until months later.

Winter 1988.

I heard a knock at the Brooklyn office's front door and opened it. Part of my job. Several young dudes with country accents barged in.

"I'm K-Ci and that's my brother Jo-Jo."

"I'm Devante."

"I'm Devante's brother, Dalvin."

"And who's that?" I asked, pointing at the fifth person in

the bunch.

"He's our cousin."

"Are ya'll a new group signed to Uptown?" I asked.

"Yes, ma'am. We just met with Andre at the other office."

"Really?"

"Yes, ma'am. We were driving back to North Carolina and stopped here to meet the rest of the staff."

"The rest of the staff is downstairs, that way," I said.

"I'm staying up here with you," Dalvin said. The others trotted down the spiral stairs while Dalvin pulled up a chair beside me. That was where he remained until the rest of his crew was ready to hit the road. "Here's my business card," Dalvin said before dashing out the door. "Call me."

"Okay," I said.

Spring 1989.

The two sets of brothers were back in the Big Apple, but this time to stay. They were ready to embark on a new career—a career that ultimately took them around the world as one of the most memorable R&B groups, Jodeci. But before that moment arrived, Dalvin, Devante, K-Ci, JoJo, and their cousin met me at the Brooklyn office early Sunday morning, May 21, 1989. I will never forget the date. How could I? It was on my twenty-seventh birthday.

Sandra, the office manager, had asked me to open up shop in her stead since I happened to be living in a small room at the YWCA within walking distance. I agreed. The guys were to meet up with Andre Harrell at the Brooklyn office and from there Andre would take them to their new home. When I arrived at the office around nine o'clock in the morning, they were packed in a van in front of the office. They'd been parked out there all night long, they told me.

Once inside Dalvin was back in my face to pick up where he had last left off. Trust me when I say I had no objection. The boy was fine, and I was eager to be in his company, too.

"Why didn't you call me, Vanessa?" he asked.

"I don't know."

Andre arrived around noon. Shortly thereafter we all hopped into the two whips parked out front. Devante and I rode with Andre in his black jeep and the rest of the guys rode in the van they'd driven from Charlotte. When we pulled up in front of a housing project in the Bronx, I was taken aback. For some reason I expected a big, fancy house somewhere in New Jersey. The guys unloaded their luggage and we made our way onto a pissy elevator that took us up to an untidy apartment, an apartment that once housed Andre and his family.

After we took a quick tour around their new dwelling, we all ended up in one of the small bedrooms. Dalvin grabbed one of his bags and proceeded to empty the contents onto the floor.

"Wait, Dalvin!" I said. "Let me sweep up this trash before you dump all those sneakers on the floor." While I swept the room with a broom I found in the kitchen, Andre gave the guys a little pep-talk.

"Are you all going to be okay?" Andre asked at the end.

"Yes, sir! We'll be just fine with Vanessa here with us," Dalvin blurted out.

"Good. I'm out," said Andre.

"Do ya'll have money for food?" I asked the guys as Andre walked out the bedroom.

"No," they responded in unison.

"Andre, hol' up." I caught up with him in the hallway. "Can you leave some money so they can get something to eat? They don't have any food here, you know." Andre dug in his pants pocket, pulled out a twenty dollar bill, and handed it to me, then zoomed out the front door. "Andre gave me twenty bucks so ya'll can get something to eat," I said. "What do ya'll want from the store?"

"Bring back a six pack of beer," Devante said.

"What kind?"

"Heineken."

Dalvin and I left the apartment to find the nearest grocery store. We bought the beer and some other items and jetted back upstairs. Devante snatched the six pack from my hands and moved toward one of the bedrooms where Jo-Jo and K-Ci and their cousin were lounging the night away.

"Wait a minute," I said before Devante left. "Let me get a beer." I cracked open my beer, took a couple of swallows, and sat on Dalvin's lap on the living room sofa. "You don't want a beer?" I asked, not realizing I was nine years his senior.

"No, I don't drink."

Before I knew it, time had flown by. It was way past midnight and the house was quiet as a mouse, except for Dalvin, who seemed to really enjoy talking as he stood up to demonstrate each story he told. I excused myself and headed to the bathroom, only to find Devante lying on the floor.

"Ohmygod!" I cried. "Are you alive?" I nudged him with my foot. He didn't budge but let out a low moan that told me he'd drunk too much. "Dalvin!" I yelled. "Your brother is passed out on the bathroom floor and I gots to pee."

"Step over him," Dalvin yelled back.

"He's lying right in front of the toilet." I tried pushing him to one side, but he was dead weight. "Dalvin!" I yelled again. "Let's pick him up and put him in bed."

"No! Leave him there."

I could no longer hold in my piss. I somehow managed my way onto the toilet seat and quickly handled my business. After I washed my hands, I made my way back to the living room and crashed on the couch alongside Dalvin until the sun rose. When I got up to leave, Devante was still passed out on the bathroom floor.

I found my way to the nearest train station and before long was back in my room at the YWCA with just enough time to shower and change before I was due at the office to answer my first phone call of the day.

Ring…ring…ring.

“Good morning. Uptown. This is Vanessa. How may I direct your call?”

“Hey, Vanessa. Dis Dalvin. I’m coming down to the office to hang out with you.”

“Okay. See you when you get here.”

Chapter Twelve

My plan was to *slowly* work my way up the ladder, one step at a time, while learning all the ins and outs of the music game. My plans drastically changed, however, a few months after my start date.

Ring…ring…ring.

"Good morning. Uptown. This is Vanessa. How may I direct your call?"

"Vanessa, this is Andre. What up money?"

"Ain't nothing up."

"Vanessa, you're not the receptionist anymore."

"Huh?"

I was bewildered. I knew I was doing an excellent job. Andre had told me so himself. *Why is he taking my job away from me? I love my job.* All of a sudden I understood the meaning of Leslie's visit to the office approximately thirty minutes before Andre's call.

"Hi, how can I help you?" I had asked Leslie as she plopped her petite frame into a chair in the reception area.

"I work here now," Leslie replied.

"You work here? Right now?"

"Yup, Andre hired me."

"He hired you to do what?"

"I don't know."

"What do you know how to do?"

"Nothing. I ain't worked in over ten years."

The only job that required knowing nothing or very little was my job. I asked each employee if they knew about Leslie. They all said no. Leslie made absolutely no sense, which told me something underhanded was taking place. I questioned her some more, but the only other information I got from her was that she was the sister of Andre's girlfriend. That's when Andre called to set the record straight.

"You're the publicist now," Andre said. "I want you to train Leslie to be a great receptionist like you. And by the way, I'm taking you out to lunch tomorrow."

Andre also told me that my new salary was an extra $5,000 annually, and then hung up. After that kind of phone call I was supposed to be elated. So why wasn't I? The general manager wasn't happy either. As a matter of fact, he was fuming mad. He stormed out of the office in a rage the moment he got word I was the new Director of Publicity. As far as he could see I didn't deserve it because, unlike him, I didn't go to Yale and Columbia School of Law. In his eyes

I was nothing more than a two-bit, uneducated ghetto girl who had no rights in that capacity. And he made sure to often remind me of that. Plus, he had promised one of his lady friends that the publicist position was hers. And, oh yeah, my promotion also meant he could no longer boss me around, which he greatly enjoyed. Andre was the only one I had to answer to. Yay!

The next day I hooked up with Andre at the Manhattan office. Shortly thereafter, he and I walked to a nearby Japanese restaurant to celebrate my new job. As I sat across from Andre, I thought about telling him how uncomfortable I felt taking on this job as the head of the publicity department. He seemed excited about being able to give me this great opportunity, so I said nothing. I just sipped on my glass of red wine and ate the Sushi I had ordered while Andre made small talk and asked me a question about my children.

"Do your children have the same father?"

"Yes."

I wondered what it mattered to him whether or not my children had the same father, but I didn't ask.

After lunch, which lasted about forty-five minutes, we hopped in a yellow cab that Andre flagged down. I had no idea where we were going. Ten minutes later we ended up in a jewelry store. I thought Andre was going to buy me some bling bling to go with my new position, but that was hardly the case. Andre simply wanted to exchange his 9,000 dollar watch for a 10,000 dollar watch.

"What's wrong with that watch?" I asked, pointing at the watch he wore on his wrist.

"It's too gaudy."

Andre glanced at the fake gold watch I was wearing. I tried to hide it. At that moment I felt like such a bum in my old worn out clothes standing next to Andre who was dressed to the nines. He didn't say anything about my watch nor did he act as though he was better or richer than me but still, I felt poor next to my sort of nerdy looking, but very handsome, twenty-nine year old boss. I think the glasses he wore, and the fact that he was a tad chubby, gave him that nerdish look. But it was all good.

As Andre paid the extra G for his new watch, I thought about all the things I could buy with 10,000 bucks: a down payment on a house, new clothes for me and my children…

The next day the members of Jodeci stopped by the Brooklyn office. They congratulated me on my new position and then JoJo pulled me to the side and asked, "Who did you sleep with to get this job?" Before I had the chance to tell him, "I don't roll like that" he answered his own question. He told me I had sex with the general manager.

"I did not!"

"Yes you did."

"I did not!"

"Yes you did. You know how I know?"

"How?"

"He [general manager] told us something about you that led us to believe you had sex with him."

"What did he say?"

JoJo refused to tell me what was said so I sucked my teeth and rolled my eyes at him. It was clear to me that nothing I said would convince him that I never had sex with that low down dirty general manager. As a matter of fact, I was celibate and would remain that way throughout my tenure at Uptown and several years after. Further, if I wasn't celibate, I would have had sex with Dalvin 'cause that's who I was digging at that time.

I brushed off what JoJo said and wondered what the heck I was going to do in my new role.

In my own eyes I lacked everything needed to pull off this skyscraping gig. I wasn't an assertive bitch. I didn't cuss out folk who needed me to cuss they asses out. Instead, I allowed them to shit all over me. I didn't have the right clothes to at least look the part. I was inarticulate. And to top it all off, I had no public relations experience. The only thing I knew was that publicists set up interviews between artists and reporters. And I'd only found that out during my tenure at *Class Magazine*. Before that I'd never even heard the word publicist.

Oh! I did learn one other thing at *Class*: publicists threw nice parties. At least Simo Doe did.

Chapter Thirteen

Simo Doe was the publicist for Atlantic Records. I was her favorite contact person at *Class Magazine*. She made it her business to invite me to her fancy events, and she made sure I got an opportunity to interview some of Atlantic Records' hottest recording artists. When she witnessed me behaving like a groupie, which slipped out occasionally, she didn't hesitate to give me good advice about what not to do in the music game, if I wanted to last long in it.

I appreciated her frankness and constructive criticism. She was a tad uppity but real. I liked that about her—the real part. I liked her style, too. She was professional and classy and always well dressed. That's the kind of publicist I wanted to be when the time was right. The time wasn't right, but it was here. I just wasn't ready...Mentally.

I vividly remember the album release party Simo threw for Miki Howard, one of Atlantic Records' artists. It was held

November 19, 1986, at Stringfellows, a New York City night club on 21st Street in Manhattan.

I carefully observed the way Simo stood at the door and greeted each invited guest. She knew them all by name. I remember the way she made me feel as I walked through that door and was greeted by her "happy to see you" smile. She made me feel special, like I was somebody important, as she welcomed me into the club and handed me a wonderfully made small shopping bag filled with Miki Howard promotional items.

Once I was inside the club, Miki spotted me, seized my hand, and asked if I wanted to grab a seat at one of the tables so I could finish interviewing her.

"No," I said. "I got my story."

Rewind.

Earlier that day Miki sort of dissed me at the Sheraton Hotel where she was staying while in New York. I'm sure it wasn't premeditated, but all the same she dissed me.

Simo, as was her custom, set up an interview between Miki and me. "Meet us at the Sheraton at four o'clock," she told me over the phone. When I arrived, Simo introduced me to Miki, who sat at a table in the hotel's restaurant. Right after that Simo bounced. I joined Miki at her table as a waiter brought over a pot of tea she'd ordered. She wore a T-shirt and slacks and, if I'm not mistaken, slippers, or what looked liked slippers. Her hair was untidy and she wore no make-up. She looked like she'd just woken up. In spite of that she was pretty, a natural beauty.

"You want some tea?" she asked me.

"Sure," I said. I poured tea into my cup and added a couple of scoops of sugar. Then I gave my tea a stir before I took a sip.

"Come on! Come on! Hurry up!" Miki barked. She seemed anxious to go back to her room, so I reached in my purse, whipped out my sixty-dollar machine, pressed record, and threw out some questions that she graciously and quickly answered. Then, just like Doug E. Fresh, Miki had a question of her own to ask me.

"How old are you?"

"Twenty-four."

"You're my age!" Miki said. "I thought you were a high school kid."

"Yes, I get that a lot."

I squeezed in one more question before Miki jumped out of her seat. "I gotta go," she said, kissing my neck, then jetted off.

Left alone, I took a few more sips of my tea and wondered who was responsible for the tab. *What's the protocol?* Whatever it was, I wasn't going to pay for all that tea, nor leave a tip. I couldn't. My pockets were bare. I didn't have any money on me except a token to ride the train back to my hood on 164th Street, where I lived at the time.

I looked around the room and saw the waiter who'd served

the tea, a tall, dark-haired young white guy. He was paying attention to a customer across the room. This was my chance to flee, in case I was responsible for the bill. I got up and casually walked toward the entrance, looking straight ahead, hoping I didn't get that tap on the shoulder and, "Excuse me, Miss, you forgot to pay."

Chapter Fourteen

In my new position as head of the publicity department, I did nothing except drift around sadly as self-doubt and fear overwhelmed me.

Who was going to teach me how to be the top-notch publicist Andre imagined I'd be? I suggested spending time with Simo Doe in order to learn her ways. Andre wasn't feeling her. He suggested Juanita Stephen—publicist for MCA Records—believing she was the better publicist to show me the ropes. He thought she had more experience with hip hop artists. Simo really didn't deal much with rappers, if at all.

Andre sort of made arrangements for me to hang out with Juanita. I attended one photo shoot she arranged for Heavy D and the Boyz. After that, a coworker whispered in my ear. "Juanita said she does not want you watching her work." That was all I needed to hear. I never went around Juanita again.

As the weeks went by I continued to do absolutely nothing. I gradually changed from Miss Happy-Go-Lucky to Miss Down-and-Out. It was becoming apparent to others that I wasn't the same bubbly go-getter that I was before my promotion, that someone who had somehow convinced Andre I was right for the job. I felt like Sissy Spacek in the movie *Carrie*, when her character tells her religiously fanatic mother that she wants to go to the prom. Her mother scolds her and says, "They're all going to laugh at you!"

What bothered me most, however, was that I let Andre down. I made him look like an idiot for promoting me. He was an idiot, some may say. Idiot or not, he was simply trying to take a sister to a higher level in the music game because he saw something in her that she didn't see in herself. And for that I would be forever grateful. But in the meantime, I was sorry it wasn't working out.

Chapter Fifteen

While I was failing miserably as the company's publicist, nineteen-year-old Puffy, who's known as P. Diddy today, was quickly soaring in his new position as head of the A&R (artists and repertoire) department, a position he obtained a few weeks after my promotion. Before that he was the company's intern, a flashy-dressing inspiring dancer who wore vests and cute little ties.

"Vanessa, can you write a bio for me?" Puffy asked when I was the underpaid receptionist. He must've heard through the wire that I was a writer. "I'm a dancer in a group."

"Nope, not gon' do it. I'm not doing nothing no more except answer the phone."

"Come on, Vanessa. Please."

"Nope! I'm not doing nothing else extra around here until Andre pays me more money."

I can still remember the day Heavy D had a party at his home in Mount Vernon. I had never been to Mount Vernon before, nor did I have a clue how to get out there. "I'll take you to the party," an unknown visitor at the Brooklyn office told me.

I made contact with Dalvin, who had become one of my hangout partners, and told him I got us a ride and to gather up his band mates and meet me at the Manhattan office.

"We don't have money to get down there," Dalvin said.

"Hop the train."

"What if we get caught?"

"Ya'll are going to jail if you get caught. So don't get caught."

I felt bad advising them to sneak on the subway, but that was how everybody I knew did it when short on cash. It was the New York way. Thankfully, they pulled it off. The last thing I needed was for them to end up in jail on account of my bad advice.

When the unknown visitor and I pulled up in front of Uptown's Manhattan office building on 57th Street in his Yugo car, I wasn't expecting to see Puffy standing in front of the building, too. *How in the heck are seven people going to fit in this small car?*

Dalvin sat up front with me and the driver. Puffy and the other three members of Jodeci tried with all their might to squeeze in the back seat, to no avail. Somebody was going to have to crouch down in the car's storage compartment, and it wasn't going to be me. When I looked over my shoulder and saw that Puffy had somehow squeezed his thin frame into the seat behind me, I knew it wasn't going to be him either.

On the ride to Mount Vernon, we all giggled when we caught a glimpse of K-Ci curled up like a newborn baby in the tiny storage compartment, protesting the whole way.

Until my promotion, Puffy and I were a lot alike and Puffy made it his business to tell me so minutes after we all ended up in Heavy's backyard. "I like you," Puffy told me. "You're just like me: a go-getter." And just like me, Puffy caught Andre's attention. Just like me, Puff showed up at nearly every New York City industry party. When possible, he even made it his business to walk into a party in the arms of a famous person (e.g. Rosie Perez at the *Do the Right Thing* party). He knew photographers would be snapping away at the famous person, and the person with the famous person, which could possibly land him in a magazine or two.

While Puffy was still an intern, he had the galls to request company's business cards. The general manager had a fit. He thought it was absurd for an intern to have cards so he bitched about it. I don't know if Puffy got those cards at that time, but I'm certain he did upon his promotion.

Chapter Sixteen

After a couple months Andre knew he had to do something about my situation. So an all-employee evaluation was set up in the boardroom of the Manhattan office. No one had to tell me. I knew this was the day I would be set free from my job as deadbeat publicist. When it was my turn to enter the boardroom, I overheard some of my coworkers whispering and laughing. Then one of them chanted out loud as I walked past with my head down, "Somebody's getting fire! Somebody's getting fire!"

I sat at a long table in the midst of Andre, the general manager, and Steve Lucas, another executive. For the first time since my big promotion I didn't have butterflies in my stomach. I felt relieved. I knew my high-powered position was finally over. But Andre didn't seem to know how to tell me.

Everyone sat around the table looking kind of stupid. When the general manager, who'd irked my nerves since the day I got promoted, made a few unintelligent comments, I stared him down for a good long minute. Then I rolled my eyes at him.

"She's insubordinate!" he cried out.

I shook my head at him, sucked my teeth, then turned to Andre.

"You talk," I said. "You're the boss."

Without hesitating Andre said, "I want you to be my assistant."

I didn't hesitate either. "Okay. I want to be your assistant."

"I want you to start tomorrow. Be here at ten o'clock."

"Tomorrow?!" I cried out. "Me and Elaine Wood were planning on going to Atlanta for the Jack the Rapper convention. Can I start when I get back?"

"No! You can't go to Jack the Rapper. I want you here tomorrow at ten o'clock and don't be late."

I was a little bummed about not being able to go. Elaine and I had spent all week planning the trip. Now she'd have to go by herself. Oh well. At least I was still employed at Uptown Records. And as far as I was concerned, Jack the Rapper couldn't beat that.

My new position brought new pay. Another $5,000 was added to my annual salary, which left me wondering if I had been demoted or promoted. My new job title, Executive Administrative Assistant, told me I was demoted, but my pay raise said otherwise.

I finally copped my own place, too. Sort of. Michael, an associate of mine, suggested I sublet his one-bedroom Brooklyn apartment in a brownstone on Hoyt Street, when I had informed him I was sort of homeless.

"Six fifty per month and it's all yours."

I got my children from Millie, who still lived with her sister in Manhattanville Housing Projects, and we moved in. I enrolled them into a nearby school and carried on in my new job until I got a phone call that would change the course of my life.

Chapter Seventeen

"Hold on, Elaine, that's my other line," I said.

"Vanessa, this is Andre."

My heart fell to the floor. It was Thursday evening and I hadn't reported to work since last Friday. And it'd only been a couple months since I'd started my new job.

"Hi, Andre. What's up?"

"I'm letting you go, Vanessa."

"Why?" I asked, trying to sound clueless.

"You're not doing what I want you to do. I didn't give you permission to take a vacation."

"I know, but I needed one. I left you a note saying I was on vacation for a week. I was coming back to work on Monday."

"I'll tell you what. You can go back to being the receptionist at the Brooklyn office, and I'm reducing your salary."

"No, Andre, I can't do that."

"Okay. You can pick up your severance pay tomorrow."

Going back to being the receptionist in Brooklyn meant going back to work under the general manager. Oh heck to the no! Even though it was I who had sabotaged my new position, I knew going back would be totally humiliating. No way could I hold my head high after being dropped from publicist all the way back down to receptionist. I was already dealing with the embarrassment of being dropped from publicist to secretary. Thanks, but no thanks.

Devastated! I clicked back over to see if Elaine was still holding. Yep, she sure was. Too distraught to continue my conversation with her, I gave her a lame excuse about why I had to end the call and said goodbye.

The next day my children and I walked to the Brooklyn office to get my severance pay. The general manager was delighted to be the one to give it to me, along with a pink slip. His countenance told me so. While I was there, another employee told me that Andre hired a white girl to replace me and was paying her twice as much as he'd paid me. "And she's got her own personal assistant, too." I really didn't care to hear the extras. It did nothing but dampen my spirits.

From the Brooklyn office I strolled to the nearest unemployment office. Once that matter was squared away, my children and I hopped on the A train, which took us to East Village, where we had lunch at BBQ's.

The next week I found employment as a word processor at a small black-owned accounting firm in Brooklyn. A week later measures were taken so that I could get paid under the table, an arrangement that worked out well for both me and the employer.

Chapter Eighteen

All went well until Michael heard that I no longer worked at Uptown Records. I don't know why, but that bit of news didn't sit well with him. I could hear the hostility in his voice when he phoned me around three weeks after my termination. "Why didn't you tell me you got fired?"

I didn't know I was obligated to tell him. I thought I was only obligated to pay him rent. Whatever!

Michael was one of those fake industry friends—the ones who befriend you because of your connection to something and, when you're no longer connected to that something, drop you like a hot potato.

I was Michael's connection to Uptown Records, which, I quickly discovered, was the only reason he'd sublet his apartment to me. His new attitude told me so. It was an attitude I'd not yet met. His tone of voice was rough and unkind as he told me on a cold Sunday evening, "I want my apartment back!"

"Why?" I asked. "I just paid you the rent, Michael."

"Why didn't you tell me you got fired?" He sounded more disappointed than I about the loss of my job. "I want you out now!"

"I'm not leaving now! It's dark out there, and cold."

"Who do you think you're talking to like that?"

Michael slammed down the phone and within minutes was banging on my door. I let him in, hoping to rectify this situation that made absolutely no sense to me. Once inside he began yelling at me, demanding his apartment back. My children didn't understand his problem either. Their facial expression said, *"Why is this six-foot-plus giant yelling at my moms?"* My eleven-year-old daughter, who always became traumatized any time she saw an argument or fight, started crying as Michael ranted and raved. Her tears didn't faze him one iota.

Finally he left us alone, or so I thought. I went to the kitchen and turned on the faucet to wash the dishes. To my horror the water was scalding. I immediately phoned Michael. "What did you do to the water? What is wrong with you, dummy?" Michael's response was the same. He yelled and slammed down the phone.

Moments later the apartment went black. Then Michael was banging at my door again. Although he lived on Atlantic Avenue, which was within walking distance, I still wondered how he was able to get there so quickly, considering I'd never seen him in possession of a car. This time I didn't let him in.

He was straight tripping. "Turn the lights back on or I'm calling the police," I yelled through the door. He turned on the lights but I called the police anyway. They arrived within minutes.

Outside, Michael greeted the two white officers. He spoke with them a good ten minutes. That was a bad sign. I knew that Michael, a white man who had studied law, would make a better impression on them than I. Well, Michael was multiracial. But the white side was more prominent. A lot more.

When the officers finally came inside my apartment I told them I was the one who'd called and I didn't appreciate them talking to Michael first. I began to tell my side of the story when one of the officers cut me off and told me I had to leave. They had no interest in what I had to say. They didn't even take down a report. I was stunned! They were assisting Michael with an illegal eviction. But then again I wasn't too stunned. New York City cops were known for breaking the law and getting away with it.

"I have nowhere to go," I told the officers. "Can I stay here until tomorrow?"

"I'm sorry, miss. We need you to vacate the premises now."

"But where am I supposed to go at this time of night?"

"I don't know, miss. Do you want us to take you to a shelter?"

"Yes, I guess so."

What else was I supposed to do? I had no rental contract. It was my word against Michael's. I had no idea what story he'd told those police officers to convince them to put me and my two small children out in the dark, cold night. I had neither the familiarity with nor the know-how to deal with law-related issues like this. Only years later, while watching the *Judge Mathis Show*, would I realize that I had a strong case against Michael, that I could have sued him for an illegal eviction and intentional infliction of emotional distress upon me and my children.

I got on the phone to one of my friends, author Nathasha Brooks-Harris, and told her everything that had taken place.

"Where are you going?" she asked.

"The cops are taking us to a shelter."

"Oh, no! You do not want to go to a shelter, Vanessa. Those shelters are terrible. Come stay at my house."

Nathasha lived in a big brownstone roughly ten minutes away. I called a cab and threw into the trunk as many of our things as I could fit. I told Michael I'd be right back to gather a few more things. I also asked him if I could hold onto the key until the next day, at which time I'd return with a U-Haul to get the bigger items. He agreed. I locked the front door to the apartment. "I'll be right back, Michael," I said.

When we arrived at Nathasha's we unloaded the taxi, put our things in her house, then jumped back in to go back for our other things. When we arrived, all our belongings had been thrown into the hallway. I couldn't get into the apartment because Michael had padlocked the front door. He was nowhere to be found. I couldn't believe I'd been treated this way by a man who was once attracted to me, or pretended he was. We'd never had any run-ins. I'd never done anything to him, except invite him out to a couple concerts and parties or let him wine and dine me. His behavior made absolutely no sense to me whatsoever. It was extraordinary. That's when I began to believe that this situation was much deeper than Michael. Something in the spiritual realm was taking place, maybe some kind of lesson I was being taught. First I lost the job of my dreams and then suffered an unlawful eviction, all in less than a month.

It was late and I was too tired and stressed to deal with the big mess I was in. I told my children to look through the pile and get anything important to them because I would not return there ever again. Then we left everything else in the hallway and jumped back into the same cab to go to Nathasha's. I was so done with that part of this mess. I would deal with the other part in the morning.

My children and I arrived at Michael's residence on Atlantic Avenue bright and early the next morning. It was time for me to deal with the rent money I'd paid Michael two days before the illegal eviction.

"Unless you sign this," Michael told me as he sat behind a desk, "I am not giving you your money back." He shoved a torn-off piece of scrap paper at me. It was a handwritten contract.

I barked. "I am not signing that!"

He simply barked right back, still without a care in the world that children were looking him dead in his face as if he were a cold-hearted loony. For a moment I thought about contacting a few goons to manhandle Michael. Thankfully I didn't know any.

I just wanted my money and I was mentally tired of dealing with Michael and this big mess that had come upon me. So I signed the stupid contract that stated I would not take legal actions against him. Michael didn't even give me a copy and I didn't care. I was done with him. I was done with this whole mess that had made not only me homeless again, but my children, too.

We stayed with Nathasha for about three weeks. Then I got a call from my sister. She was so excited.

"Guess what?" she said.

"What?"

"I got accepted into the projects."

I was just as excited, if not more. "When can we move in?"

She told me it was going to take a week before housing gave her the key to her very first apartment. I knew the Most High's hand was wrapped up in this because that same day Nathasha asked me what my next move was going to be. I knew that meant I was wearing out my welcome and it was time to bounce elsewhere. I asked her if I could stay one more week until my sister got the key. She agreed.

What a glorious day for us all when we moved into the Dyckman Housing Projects. We couldn't have cared less that we had to sleep on the floor the first few weeks because we had no furniture. We all lived happily together for five months, and then I was accepted into a two-bedroom income based apartment on Linden Boulevard and Nostrand Avenue in Brooklyn. All praises to the Creator of the Heavens and Earth. I, too, finally had my first *real* apartment.

Millie stayed with her sister a little while longer and eventually she too was accepted into an income based apartment in Harlem, on 114th Street.

My brother was still incarcerated.

Chapter Nineteen

Months after my termination from Uptown Records, Elaine and I attended a party thrown by Def Jam Records. While there I spotted my former boss, Andre Harrell. Even though he'd fired me, I never held a grudge or became bitter toward him. Why would I? It was my doing that got me terminated as his assistant, so I was never angry with him for doing what he felt he had to do to show me who was the boss.

I was happy to see him and he seemed happy to see me. As I gave him a big bear hug, Michael walked past. I could tell Michael was shocked to see me wrapped around the stocky man who'd fired me. Andre noticed that we didn't speak to each other.

"What's up with that?" he asked. I briefly told him about the illegal eviction. Then he popped the question.

"You want your high seat back, Vanessa?"

"High seat? What's a high seat?"

"My assistant. Do you want your job back as my assistant?"

I couldn't believe it! *Is he for real?* I wondered. *Is he really going to hire me back? What about that white girl he hired to replace me?* I didn't know what to say. Inside I said, *You damn skippy I want my job back!* But when I opened my mouth to respond, "No" escaped, loud, clear, and proud.

Chapter Twenty

Spring 1992.

My love for the music game was still strong. I wanted back in. I submitted my resume to Zomba-Jive Records, the label of Britney Spears, R. Kelly, and a slew of other platinum-selling artists. Not long after, I was hired by Barry Weiss, the general manager at that time. He hired me right over the phone, site unseen.

"You sure you don't have any other positions available?" I asked.

"No, that's all we have a need for right now."

I swallowed my pride and accepted the position as the company's switchboard operator. I figured once in, I'd worm my way into another position. Life at Zomba was no match for the good times I'd had at Uptown Records, but at least I was back in the game. I got along fairly well with my new co-workers. Everything was all good, especially the times R. Kelly popped up and made my heart melt.

"I like your outfit," I told Kelly one of those times. He had on a two-piece pajama-like outfit with a stocking cap to match. It was unique.

"Thank you," he said. He seemed bashful at first, nothing at all like the person I had seen humping around on stage.

"It's real nice," I continued. Then all of a sudden he walked closer to my station and looked me up and down.

"You're a cutie," he said.

"Thanks." I carried on with the zillion and one phone lines, pretending as though his flattering remark was no biggie. If only he knew: I was blushing inside.

The good times at Zomba came to an immediate halt when Uptown Records' general manager—I mean, former general manager—found out I worked there. He popped in nearly every day, grinning in my face, acting like he and I were ace-coon-boon the way we used to be during the early stages of my tenure at Uptown. He told me that he had applied for employment at Zomba but to no avail. He even suggested that he and I start a business together. Imagine that. "No!" I told him. "All you ever do is put me down."

He began making friends with the employees I spent most of my time around. Maybe it was a coincidence, but every last one of those employees stopped speaking to me, all at the same time. Whatever the true reason my co-workers turned against me, I assumed Uptown's former general manager was behind it after all, he had a history of trying to sabotage my relationships and reputation.

One morning I reported to work and one of my co-workers accused me of being late. A couple days before that, one had accused me of something else. Days before that another laughed, whispered, and pointed at me every time I walked past her. I knew that I was being set up. I wasn't up for the fight. I wasn't going to subject myself to their attacks another day.

I wrote a *thank-you-for-the-opportunity-but-sorry-I-quit* note to Barry Weiss and placed it in his office before he arrived that morning and I walked off the job, leaving the switchboard unattended. I didn't say anything to anyone. I just walked off.

I was done with that drama! Not only was I done with Zomba-Jive Records, I was done with New York City, too.

August 1993.

I packed up my children and whatever else I could fit into my friend's Jetta and waved good-bye as we drove into the sunset to start a brand new life in the South.

Part III

Sleeping with the Enemy

Chapter Twenty-One

[1]Lucifer and I met in Atlanta, Georgia, a year after I'd settled into a one-bedroom apartment on Covington Highway in Decatur. This was the first time I had lived in or seen an apartment complex with a swimming pool, lake, and tennis and racket courts, among other things. For a little over four hundred bucks per month rent, I thought I was living large with two walk-in closets, a dishwasher, a crystal chandelier in the dining area, and a balcony. I pictured myself living in something like this in New York. No way I'd have gotten all that for that price. No siree! In New York something like that would cost a good grand and a half, if not more, and the apartment would be a lot smaller and probably include beady-eyed mice.

I wanted to share my new beautiful life with my sister—who was still living in Dyckman projects with her four

---

[1] Name has been changed.

children, struggling to kick a drug habit she had acquired—so I called her and told her to join me. She was elated and so was I. We both agreed: new and different scenery was what she needed to kick her habit. My sister and her youngest child joined me a couple weeks later. She retrieved the rest of her children, who were in Millie's care, upon obtaining her own apartment a few months later. Today my sister is still a resident of Georgia and drug free.

When Lucifer and I met, he was kind and charming and came on to me like a whirlwind. Within two months we were living together. Since I'd never shacked up with a man before, I had no clue what I was in for. Soon we were arguing every day. Two years later we were sitting in the county jail, arrested for simple battery against each other. We spent a few hours in holding cells before we were bailed out. The case was later dismissed.

Strike one.

Chapter Twenty-Two

Not surprisingly my relationship with Lucifer didn't improve. In fact, it stressed me out to the ceiling. I became increasingly depressed. I got sick on a regular basis. My back ached all the time. My hair started falling out and looking scrappy. My weight spiraled down to 96 pounds. I was totally drained and it showed.

I couldn't take this way of living any longer, always walking on eggshells while looking over my shoulder. I had to constantly watch my back because Lucifer was relentlessly scheming, looking for different ways to hold me down. When I was sad, it made Lucifer glad. When I was glad, it made Lucifer mad. Life with him turned me into someone I didn't know or like. *What happened to that energized, happy person I was a year before meeting Lucifer?* I wanted her back. Something had to give. I wanted my power back, too. I knew there was something about Lucifer that kept sucking it all out. My inner voice kept telling me he wanted the worst for me by any means necessary. I knew I had to get away from him, but every time I tried something pulled me back.

In February 1997 I mustered the strength to leave him. I waited until he went to work one evening before calling a moving truck. I wanted to leave in peace, and with Lucifer around that was out of the question. On that particular day I made it my business to be extra nice to him, including giving him a little nookie that morning.

I think Lucifer had started to suspect I was making plans to leave him. He noticed some of my dishware missing from the cubbyhole—dishware that I'd been stashing, little by little, into the new apartment I'd secretly acquired weeks before. He started leaving for work and then an hour later creep back into the house, claiming he'd decided not to go that day. But I caught on to what he was doing. I knew the little nookie trick would convince him that all was good between us and he'd feel secure enough to keep his butt at work all night. It worked.

I didn't see Lucifer until the next day, when I spotted him on a pay phone at the Belvedere Shopping Plaza as I drove down Columbia Drive, my son in the passenger seat. Not wanting a confrontation, I made a U-turn. Too late. Lucifer saw me, too, and leaped in his car. The chase was on and popping. He chased me like a maniac, ignoring every red light. I turned right on Memorial Drive, Lucifer on my tail and barely missing other vehicles. I was frightened and prayed he'd crash. *What the heck is he trying to do?* My legs shook uncontrollably while I drove as fast and as safely as possible to the nearest police station. There wasn't an officer in sight. I jumped out of my whip and ran to the door. It was locked.

"Help!" I screamed, banging on the door.

Two young, black, male officers finally appeared. When Lucifer saw them he jumped out of his whip.

"She's got a warrant!" he yelled before I could speak.

"Ma'am, we have to check to see if you have a warrant," one of them said.

Once they verified there was a warrant out for me, I was told to put my hands behind my back and I was cuffed right in front of my son. I hated for him to see me like that. But more than that, I was going to jail for the second freakin' time.

Lucifer gloated from ear to ear as the officers took me inside the precinct, my son tagging along. I was placed in one of those cell blocks with vertical bars. My son was allowed to talk to me through the bars until my sister came and got him and my car.

Later that day I was transported to Dekalb County Jail, where I met the detective assigned to my case.

"Why was I arrested?" I asked the detective.

"He said you were homeless. He offered you a place to live, and this is the thanks he got. You robbed him."

"Whaaaaaaat?!" I yelled. "He said I was homeless and what?"

"Here." The detective shoved a pad and pen at me. "Write down what happened."

Charged with "theft by taken," I remained locked up for seventy-two hours before I was released on my own recognizance. The case was dismissed two months later but not before the judge threatened to make Lucifer pay a fine for perjury and for playing games with the judicial system.

Strike two.

Chapter Twenty-Three

Instead of suing Lucifer for malicious prosecution, I got back together with him after dismissal of the case. But we continued to live in separate dwellings. This gave Lucifer ample freedom to know other women, which led to the day when I became one of *them*. You know the kind. A Gormless-Drama-Queen-Twit.

It happened one balmy summer evening, August 2, 1999. I was lounging on Lucifer's living room sofa, watching the six o'clock news while gobbling a home-cooked plate of soul food, when she stood in front of me, hands propped on her hips, and yelled, "Get out, heifer!" She was one of the women Lucifer got to know while he and I were living in separate homes.

"This is not your house, sweetie," I calmly replied. "You get out."

"You getting the fuck out of this house, bitch. He's my man now!"

"I can't tell."

The little spat escalated to home girl going through the bag of personal items I'd put in one of the bedrooms. She took the items out of my bag one by one and threw them out of the bedroom onto the floor in the hallway.

"You getting the fuck out of this house, bitch," she yelled a few more times while continuing to toss my belongings.

I heard my new sweet-smelling expensive bottle of perfume crash into tiny pieces as it hit the floor. She was like a mad woman—mad with jealousy. I knew exactly where she was trying to take this thing, so I waited for Lucifer to intercede. After all, I was there for him and not her. She was his problem, not mine. So I expected him to man up and rectify his problem. He acted as though he had nothing to do with the situation taking place before his eyes. He picked up the cordless phone, stepped over my belongings on the floor, and out the front door he went. Now what was I supposed to do with his problem that had turned into my problem? My inner voice told me to get the heck out of that house. *Leave, Vanessa. Now!*

Ignoring my inner voice I sat my plate of food on the coffee table, then straightened my Gormless-Drama-Queen crown. I had to make sure that bad boy was propped up just right on my head before I showed this aggravating hussy a thing or two about messing with me.

"I'm sick of you, you stupid ass crack ho," I said as my index finger found its way to her forehead to poke at it while

I gave her a piece of my mind. Then the fight was on and cracking. By the time Lucifer came back, she was losing a lot of blood from the deep gash my Swiss Army knife had given her.

"Call an ambulance!" Lucifer shouted as he stood between me and her while keeping his eyes on me, afraid I would use my knife again.

By this time I was hardly thinking about her. The only thing on my mind was getting the heck out of there before the police came. For a moment Lucifer averted his eyes and I grabbed my purse. I almost lost my footing on the bloody, slippery floor before getting out the front door. As for my belongings she'd thrown on the floor, I'd worry about that later.

My car was parked in front of the house, but it wouldn't start. *Bummer!* I walked down the driveway, stashing my knife in my pants pocket, my Gormless-Drama-Queen crown still propped up nice. I had represented well for all the Gormless-Drama-Queen-Twits around the world fighting some woman over some gormless man.

Now what? I asked myself.

Now what? Now you're in a world of trouble, that's what. You sure showed her!

As I walked down the driveway, considering my next move, Lucifer came up behind me. "You gotta leave, now! Get away from—" And there she came, running down the driveway, yelling obscenities like a maniac. Her grave injury must've slipped her mind when she saw Lucifer close to me. "He's *my* man. Get away from him!" She swung her arms like an out-of-control octopus. Lucifer wrapped his fat arms around my upper body, squeezing my own arms to my sides. Now I was pissed.

"Get off me!" I screamed, trying to wiggle from his grip. His hold tightened, immobilizing me. I could barely breathe.

"Get back in the house," Lucifer yelled at her. "Call the ambulance!"

She paid him no mind and tried to get at me over his big fat body. *Please call an ambulance, dummy*, I said to myself—not because I cared, but because I didn't want murder on my hands. While trying to get at me, she pushed Lucifer. But that didn't break his tight hold. He and I tumbled to the pavement. Then I was laid out flat on my back and he threw his heavy body on my stomach. His hands pinned my arms to prevent me from slashing her again, I presumed. But I had no intention of using my knife on her again. Like I said, I didn't want murder on my hands. All I wanted was to leave, get my thoughts together, and figure out my next move.

I twisted under Lucifer's heavy body, bronco-riding and squashing me at the same time, while she still tried to swing at me. A few of her baby punches landed on Lucifer's head. I chuckled to myself.

"Call the ambulance!" Lucifer yelled again, ducking her soft blows. Finally she went back in the house. Finally

Lucifer lifted his fat body off me. Without his help I picked myself up, brushed dirt off my clothes and out of my Afro, and scurried away. To save time I cut across the grass. I heard Lucifer on the cordless phone. "She's wearing a brown shirt and gray shorts." I walked faster, trying to figure out which way the police would come so I could go in the opposite direction. I took my knife out of my pocket and threw it in a bush. Within minutes the police pulled up beside me.

"Are you the one that got stabbed?" asked a female officer. "Who did this to you? Are you hurt?" Without waiting for a response she told me to get in the back of her patrol car and drove me back to the scene. At the house she let me out of the car, still under the impression that I was the injured party. After all I did have blood on my hands and clothes.

The officer left me unattended until she got a statement from Lucifer, who sat on his patio pretending to console his other Gormless woman. When the officer zoomed down the driveway and approached me with a brand new attitude, it was obvious Lucifer had ratted me out. She grabbed my wrist, twisted me around, and threw me up against the car. "Put your other hand behind your back," she barked. I halfheartedly did it. She helped me out and cuffed my wrists. "Spread your legs!" She frisked me and searched my purse. "Where's the knife?"

"I don't know. I dropped it."

"Where?"

"I don't know."

After she read me my rights I was placed in the back of her police car. I felt so dumb sitting there, my Gormless-Drama-Queen crown now tilted to the side. I looked out the window just as an ambulance pulled up. I saw the medics place Lucifer's other Gormless-Drama-Queen-Twit on a gurney, strap her in place, and hook her to an IV before placing her in the ambulance. Then I looked at Lucifer as his gormless ass stood on his patio, proud and heroic, and realized she and I must've been completely out of our minds to fight over him. What a bunch of gormless idiotic twits we all were!

Three strikes—you're out! I told myself as the officers drove me from the gory scene.

Part IV

State Property

Chapter Twenty-Four

Each cell door in pod 300 is orange (like my ugly jail suit), steel, and hefty. Half is consumed by a thick, unbreakable window with no blinds or curtains. Anyone can look inside and see your business. A switch in the control booth locks and unlocks them.

When Miss Half Pint closes cell 301 behind me, I stand by the door and give the tiny room a quick scan. Right near the entrance is a small stainless steel toilet, minus a seat. Next to that is a small stainless steel pedestal sink. On the wall above hangs a small plastic mirror, all blurry. I can barely see my face in it. At the back of the tiny cell, near a long, narrow, thick glass called a window, is a small metallic desk and chair. And in the middle of the room, pushed up against the wall, is a twin-size steel bunk with a thin, nasty looking mattress. Lying in the bottom bunk is the crazy girl I was warned about.

Her name is Jeannette Sewell. She looks a tad rough, but nothing like the burly dyke I imagined. Thank goodness! She's actually pretty. I wonder how tall she is. I guess around five feet nine and roughly a hundred ninety pounds. While I size her up, she does likewise. Then she makes it clear that I'm lucky she likes me.

"Why?" I ask.

"I usually don't like nobody they put in here. I threw all dem stank smelly bitches out. If yo' ass stank, you gots to go 'cause I don't wanna be in here smelling stank ass and pus—" She stops mid sentence to tell me I look cold and offers me a white holey t-shirt. "I like you though. You're cute. You got big pretty eyes and you don't stink, so you can stay."

"Thanks for the t-shirt." I quickly put it on under the jail outfit and wonder if I have to worry about home girl flipping out on me. I hope not because I do not feel like fighting. Fighting, after all, is the reason I'm here. The last thing I'm in need of is another charge or a beat down. And by the size of Jeannette I'm pretty sure—no, I'm positive—that my five-foot-two-inch pocketsize body will end up with the latter.

In the first few days I notice Jeannette sleeps a lot. She doesn't venture out of our cell much. Without her by my side I don't leave the cell either, except for the time I have to meet my new court-appointed counsel in the wee hours at a hearing.

The only time Jeannette goes out is chow time. She looks forward to the feedings, three times a day. Although I've made up my mind never to eat the nasty-looking food, I follow Jeannette out into the day room and get a tray of it. My sole purpose is to give my food to her. She seems to love it. I can't understand why. I bet the food tastes exactly the way it looks: disgusting.

"Ugh! What is that supposed to be?" I ask Jeannette as she gobbles every morsel.

"Shit on a shingle. You still not gon'na eat yo' food?"

"Nope. Looks like a pile of doo-doo. You want mine?"

"Hell yeah!"

Jeannette reaches across the stainless steel picnic table, grabs my brown plastic tray, and gobbles up every bit of the creamy brownish guck she calls shit on a shingle. I frown. *How can she? Yuck! I'll starve to death before I eat that nasty crap.*

At the end of the first week I'm starvin' like Marvin.

"Nah, Jeannette, you can't have my food today," I tell her as she reaches across the table for my brown tray, which has become routine. I pull the tray close, wolf down every drop of that nasty-looking shit on a shingle, and lick my fingers. I finish it off with a cup of red Kool-Aid. Ah! Refreshing!

Jeannette and I become fast friends. I learn she's kindhearted and self-sacrificing and will give you the shirt off her back, if you need it. But she doesn't seem to have any friends in our pod. I sense that most of the inmates are frightened of her, even the boyish-looking ones. I wonder if it has something to do with the rumor that she sent two inmates to Grady Hospital to get their eyes stitched up after she punched them.

I still don't come out of my cell without Jeannette by my side. I don't like the way the boyish inmates look at me—like a juicy piece of top loin steak.

Fear must be written all over my face because Jeannette says, "Don't be scared, Vanessa. I got yo' back. Anybody fuck wit you, Im'ma fuck 'em up!"

It's nice to know my back is covered but I pray that Jeannette doesn't have beef with anybody during my time here 'cause I can't promise her I've got her back, too. I don't want anymore drama added to my life. All I want is for someone to hurry up and bail me out of this joint while I'm still in one solid piece—no stab wounds, no bite marks, no scratches, no nothing.

Jeannette informs me she's a diagnosed schizophrenic. I have no clue what that means. She's on loads of medication and can seem paranoid. She believes our pod is planted with spies who are out to get her, and sometimes I think she believes I'm one of them. At other times she believes our cell has been invaded by creepy crawlers.

"Right there, Vanessa! You don't see 'em?"

"Nope. Where they at?"

"Right there on the floor."

"What do they look like, Jeannette?"

"Little black bugs. You still don't see 'em?" Jeannette squirms, screams, and hops around me, desperately trying to avoid stepping on the invisible bugs.

"Girl, you are straight bugging!" I tell her. "Ain't no bugs on the floor."

When Jeannette isn't sleeping her time away, she and I giggle and share stories about the lives we had in the free world. We even discuss the events that brought us here. I find out that, just like me, she's here because of a violent incident.

"Why did you stab them?" I ask.

"I don't know. We were all sitting on my sofa smoking crack and then I got up and went to the kitchen and grabbed the butcher knife and came back into the living room and started stabbing them for no reason."

"What did they *[two grown men]* do while you were stabbing them?"

"Dem geek monsters ran out of my house."

"Did you kill them?"

"I don't know what happen to 'em."

"How did you end up here then?"

"What happened was my daughter jumped on my back while I was stabbing them. She was trying to stop me and ended up cutting her hand on the knife. It wasn't even that serious. All she had was a tiny cut inside her hand."

"Where's your daughter?"

"The State took her and charged me with aggravated

assault and cruelty to children."

"How much time they giving you?"

"Ten years. I gotta serve one year in prison and the rest on probation."

Jeannette also tells me about the time she knocked on her neighbor's door. When he opened it, she stabbed him multiple times with a screw driver.

"Ohmygod! Why did you do that?"

"I don't know." She giggles. "He was such a nice old man, too."

It becomes clearer what it means to be schizophrenic. No wonder she's the only inmate in our pod not allowed to have a razor. Too late! Silly me already gave her one. And I'm not about to ask her for it back, especially when I see how excited she is to be able to finally shave her armpits and coochie. I silently pray, nonetheless, she doesn't have one of her moments and use the razor on me for no reason.

Week two. Nobody's come to bail me out. What's up with that? Don't my peoples know I'm at my wits' end in this zoo? I call Millie collect to remind her that my bail is set at ten G's and that ten percent of that is all I need for bail.

"We're gathering the money together, Fluffy," Millie tells me. "Your sister should be down at the jail within a day or two to bail you out. Hang in there."

Week three. I finally hang out in the dayroom without

Jeannette by my side. I make friends with some of the other inmates, especially those who make it known they're from New York. I get together with them and reminisce about life in the Big Apple. One of my favorites is Toi. Although she's ten years younger than I am, we know lots of the same people. She loves starting arguments with other inmates, though. She seems to get a kick out of it. She laughs when she tells me she didn't dare pull this crap in Riker's Island, a New York City jail.

"Why not?" I ask.

"New York girls are rough; they will slice and dice you up with the quickness."

Sierra, a bona fide crackhead, is another inmate I grow fond of, although she's not from New York. She tells me all about her life before crack. She tells me she's a mother and wife to an affluent white man who's threatening to leave her if she doesn't get her act together. She shows me pictures of how she used to look before crack jacked her up. I'm shocked. The woman I'm sitting next to is undernourished. She has black patches around sunken eyes that make her look like a raccoon. Her hair and dark skin are desiccated. The woman in the pictures is healthy and well-dressed, posing in front of a big house.

"Wow!" I say. "Is that you? You look good. Is that your house? You are living large, girl."

"My husband is getting sick of me. If I don't stop getting high, I'm going to lose him and my kid."

Sierra's time at Dekalb County Jail is short lived. She gets transported to prison a few days later.

Week five. I'm still locked up. Another public defender, Duana Sanson, has been assigned my case. Thank goodness! The first counsel sucked badly. I got this strange feeling she was not on my team. She was a bit too chummy with Detective Buice, who clearly was not on my side. If you ask me, they were in cahoots. I peeped how they were flirting with each other at the courthouse.

Duana is a pretty, dark-haired Caucasian, fairly young, and very pleasant. I sense she's on my team when she tells me she'll request a bail reduction and see if she can get my felony dropped to a misdemeanor.

I like Duana as a person but sense that she's new to the law game, possibly fresh out of law school. She seems somewhat timid and rather unrefined. But she'll have to do until I get bailed out.

After two months I wonder, *what is going on with the bail money*. My sister visits me and says they're still trying to raise bail money. She forgets to tell me that my friend Colette and one of my aunts donated money toward my bail but for some odd reason the money was spent on other things. I find this out later.

I begin to get the strangest feeling that the Creator of the Heavens and the Earth doesn't want me out just yet because nothing is making any kind of sense—a stupid fight over some bull, jail, and bail money is collected then disappears. And, oh yes. Duana is unsuccessful at getting my bail and charge reduced. *Yes! This has to be an intervention from the Creator*, I convince myself.

It's month three. While I count down the days until my sentencing, my friend Colette contacts a mutual friend, Ted Snelling. He offers to put up all the money to bail me out. The news excites me at first. But I decline his offer, hoping I'm going to be released at my sentencing, which I believe is scheduled to take place in a few days, according to Duana. I figure, *Why waste his hard-earned money that I'm sure he could use for something else more important than my stupid mess?*

To pass the time I participate in some of the activities in the dayroom while Jeannette continues to pass her time away sleeping. In the dayroom I play spades, watch TV, or watch inmates argue and fight. Sometimes I braid inmates' hair. My price is usually a honey bun or chocolate bar. Sometimes I'll accept sleeping pills.

In my cell, when Jeannette is awake, she and I usually play in the narrow window with milk cartons that she cut into the letters of the alphabet with the razor I gave her. We use the letters to communicate with the male inmates, whose windows are straight across from ours. All inmates in our pod whose narrow windows face the men participate in this activity. Communicating with men, even if they are serial killers, gang bangers, and terrorists, actually helps make our days go by more quickly, even though the conversation is usually lewd.

The male inmates always spell out the words *Show me your pussy*, and Jeannette does not hesitate to comply. She climbs on the top bunk, removes her panties, and spreads her legs for all the male inmates to see.

When the females asks the males the same thing, rows of weenies, every flavor and size, line up at the narrow windows. One weenie is so huge it actually becomes famous. It hangs out in its narrow window often.

Of course, this activity is not allowed, so we post an inmate in the dayroom as lookout. When she warns us that the on-duty correctional officer is coming, we take down the letters, which are considered contraband, and hide them under a pillow or inside a sneaker or commissary bag. Sometimes we have surprise shakedowns, when the officers barge into our cells and tear them apart, looking for contraband. If they find our letters we just collect more milk cartons during meal times and Jeannette carves again.

Month four. Jeannette confronts another inmate while hanging out in the dayroom. Officers are afraid for the other inmate and Jeannette's carried out of our pod by two big linebacker male officers. She's housed on the southeast side. I feel a tad worried without my bodyguard around. *Who's going to protect me if a big tough bully is thrown in here?*

I quickly move to the bottom bunk before a new inmate comes. After two weeks I get another cellmate. Bummer! I was enjoying the cell all to myself. My new cellmate has a horrendous odor flowing out of her coochie. Smells like a rat crawled in there and died.

"Why do you smell like that?"

"I just had an abortion," she tells me.

Abortion my ass! Whatever the issue, she's got to go! I can't do this scent another moment. Now I understand what Jeannette meant when she said she didn't tolerate smelly inmates in her cell.

I notice that my new smelly celly is friends with another inmate on the top tier, so I convince her that it would be a good idea if she moves in with her friend. She agrees. Once again I have the cell all to myself, until one week later I get another smelly cellmate. She's a Caucasian crack addict. She tells me she desperately wants to kick her drug habit and hopes she's kept in jail for several weeks. This would give her time to eat and rest. Two days go by and she's told to pack up. Her time is over and she's free to go.

"Noooo!" she cries. "I'm not ready to leave."

"Would you like to trade places with me?" I joke.

"How much time you got?"

"I haven't been sentenced yet, but it could be up to twenty years."

She reluctantly leaves the cell for the free world. I'm shocked and amazed to find inmates who in fact want to be inmates. Unbelievable!

After she leaves, the inmate in the cell next to mine asks if she can move in with me. She tells me she's afraid to be in the cell alone. Well I'm not afraid to be alone. As a matter of fact, that's exactly how I prefer it. I tell her no. Moments later I hear her screaming and banging on the door. Officers rush to her cell only to find she slit her wrist with a razor. I feel bad as they escort her to the suicidal pod.

For two more weeks I have cell 301 all to myself. How sweet it is! What would be sweeter, though, is if Duana stop telling me my court date has been pushed back. Now I wish I'd have taken Ted's offer and bailed out.

I make contact with Colette and tell her to ask Ted to reconsider bailing me out. "He spent the loot after you said not to bail you out," she says.

Chapter Twenty-Five

Now that Jeannette is out of the way, several of the boyish inmates pay my cell a visit from time to time. There is one in particular, Kimberly, who's extremely pesky at first. Every single morning she's up bright and early banging on my cell door. "Go away!" I tell her each time. I roll my eyes and suck my teeth at her, but it does no good. When I hang out in the dayroom she's always in my face, trying to convince me to bull dag with her. "I'm not gay!" I tell her over and over again. "I like men, not girls, so get lost."

Whatever I say to her must go in one ear and out the other because, like clockwork, she pursues me. I'm sick of her. Finally I stop speaking to her altogether. It helps for a short while, then she's back at it again. So I give in and befriend her. I allow her access to my cell some mornings. Then one morning, right after breakfast, she enters my cell as I sit on the bottom bunk, leans down, and kisses me smack dab on my lips. Afterward I feel a crumb or something on my lips, so I wipe my lips with the back of my hand. There it is—the thing she left on my lips—today's breakfast. A big clunk of grits. Yuck!

Another time she barges into my cell and tackles me onto my bed. While I'm flat on my back, she jumps on top of me and begins humping. "Get off!" I yell, pushing her away. I consider ignoring her again. Then I just do it. I stop speaking to her again, but this time for good.

Bummer! I finally get another cellmate. She's a boy transferred from the southeast side, where Jeannette is.

"Is your name Vanessa?" she asks me.

"Yeah, why?"

"Jeannette was my cellmate. She told me she's going to fuck me up if I mess with you."

We both have a good chuckle. And my new cellmate gives me no problems at all. *Thanks Jeannette.*

Before my new cellmate is released from jail a few days later, she tells me why she got arrested.

"I was here applying for a job as a correctional officer. When they checked my background, it showed that I had a warrant for outstanding tickets. They arrested me right on the spot."

In a matter of time another inmate will be thrown into cell 301 with me. I don't want to risk getting another smelly or psychotic one, so this time I pick my own cellmate. Or rather she picks me.

Her name is Sandra Hubbard. She's been in pod 300 about as long as I have. She's been asking me to be her celly for quite a while, but because I was enjoying those nights alone, I turned her down every time. I figure it's now or never; so I take her up on her offer. The known is better than the unknown, I reason.

Although swapping cells is against the rules, who cares? Inmates never obey jail rules. While the on-duty officer isn't paying attention, swaps take place all the time. This time it's Sandra's turn and her swap is a success.

Sandra is pretty, blonde, skinny, and close to my age. You can't tell her she's not black, though.

"I hate white people," she says.

"Excuse me? I hate to be the one to bust your bubble, but you're white, Sandra."

"No, I'm not. For real, for real."

"What you are," I chuckle, "is one crazy mess!"

Sandra is a sweetie pie. Her pimp visits her once a week and leaves ten dollars on her books every time.

"My daughter is coming to see me today," she says. "She's black."

I chuckle again. "Stop lying, Sandra."

"Yes, she is black. Wait and see. She'll be here soon."

I wait, and I see Sandra's daughter, a pretty African-American girl around eighteen years old.

"She's pretty, Sandra," I say.

"I told you she's black. I told you!"

Although I didn't ask, I wonder if Sandra's Jheri-curl-wearing pimp is her daughter's father.

Sandra loves to dance. Every day she stands by the TV in the dayroom and puts on a show. Her performances are side-splitting. This rhythmless white girl has me rolling around on the floor in tears.

Sandra also spends a lot of time chatting with one particular black male inmate in the narrow window. She thinks she's in love with him and the letter writing begins. Every single day Sandra sits on the top bunk and writes love letters to her new honey dip, in spite of the fact that she can barely read or write. But with my assistance, Sandra is able to successfully write and mail off her letters. Eventually her letter writing, or lack thereof, takes its toll on me. "I'm not gon'na keep spending my days spelling every other word for you, Sandra," I snap. "Get a dictionary!" Sandra buys a dictionary from the commissary but this still doesn't solve her issue. Duh! Silly me! Sandra is unable to find her words in the dictionary unless someone spells them. That someone is me. "Daggonit, Sandra! Sound it out. I'm tired of spelling words for you all day long. If you can't spell, then don't write any more letters!"

Month six.

Something comes over me, some type of spell. Maybe I'm

hallucinating. Maybe this is just a form of entertainment to pass the time and boredom away. Maybe this is what happens once you become a jailbird. I don't know what's happening. All I know is that I'm sitting in a small room across from my pod—the place I go whenever I want to hear the good news, break up the monotony, and hook up with Jeannette, now that she's no longer my cellmate.

The room is filled with other inmates (minus Sandra, who stays behind to chat with her honey dip in the narrow window) encircling a woman minister. I am sure her sermon is powerful, but I'm not paying attention to her. The boyish-looking inmate sitting straight across from me has my attention today. Her legs are spread wide, the way a man usually sits. Her hair, or lack thereof, is shaved close to her head, nearly bald, the way men shave their heads. I recognize her. She's the hall monitor, the special inmate who's allowed out of her pod every day, all day, to assist the on-duty correction officers. She's favored by all of them, too. As hall monitor she gets to enjoy all the advantages and privileges denied the rest of us sorry inmates.

This must be her first time attending a church service. I wonder why she decided to join us today. I never paid much attention to her until now. I examine every inch of her body, feet to head. *Is she really a female? I certainly can't tell.* My eyes make their way up to her smooth, dark-brown pretty face. And then I look into her eyes through the glasses she's wearing. She catches me staring. She stares back. I feel myself lusting after her in the same way I would lust after a man and wonder if the curse of gayness befalls one jailed after a number of days.

It is an abomination, Vanessa, to lie with a woman as with a man, my inner voice reminds me.

When church is over, I forget about what my inner voice told me. I say goodbye to Jeannette who, by the way, is shipped to prison later that day and walk over to Miss Hall Monitor, or should I call her Mister? After all, that's who she's posing as.

"Hello. How you doin'? I'm Vanessa. What's your name?"

"Yolanda. But everybody calls me Yo-Yo."

"What pod you stay in?"

"Four hundred. And you?"

"Three hundred." I hear the on-duty officer order all inmates back inside their pods. "Nice meeting you, Yo-Yo."

"Nice meeting you, too, Vanessa."

I feel Yo-Yo's eyes piercing my back as I turn from her and walk inside my pod.

After breakfast the next morning I sit down on my cot and write Yo-Yo a short letter. At the end, instead of signing my name I write "With love, cell 301."

When I see Yo-Yo mopping the hall later that day, I tell Sandra to slip the letter to her. "Don't tell her the letter's from me," I say. Sandra slides the letter under the front door while I pretend I'm totally into the game of Spades I'm playing with some of the other inmates. Yo-Yo sets the mop to the side, picks up the folded letter, and reads it. I watch as her eyes zoom in on cell 301. I chuckle to myself when I realize she has no clue the letter is from me, Miss Cell 301.

Every day for the next several days, Sandra slips Yo-Yo a letter from me. Every time I close with "With love, cell 301."

Eventually Yo-Yo figures out I'm Miss Cell 301 and writes me back. Before long we're secret lovers, daily slipping love letters back and forth to each other. When rec time rolls around, Yo-Yo and I can be found shooting hoops together. Soon Yo-Yo tells me to meet her in the mop closet. "Make like you spilled water in your cell. The officer will let you out the pod to get the mop."

In the mop closet Yo-Yo and I peck-kiss and hug. Now that I have Yo-Yo, life in jail isn't as boring. Every morning when my Maker wakes me up, I look forward to seeing Yo-Yo's face peeping inside my pod looking for me. We wave, blow kisses, and pass along our daily love letters.

Chapter Twenty-Six

April 4, 2000.

I awaken in my cell before the crack of dawn to a clicking sound. It is the on-duty correctional officer unlocking my door.

"Vanessa Murray, get up and get dressed!" she yells over the loud speaker from the control booth. "You're going to court."

I jump out of bed, brush my teeth, wash my face, and put on an ugly, wrinkled two-piece orange jail suit over my two-piece white long-john set. I slide on a new pair of white cotton socks that I bought from the commissary and then slide on my sneakers, which still have the so-called victim's blood stain on them.

Today is judgment day. Will I have to spend years behind bars or will I hear "Time served! You're free to go home, young lady"? I pray for the latter while lacing up my sneakers. I'm nervous and excited at the same time. I'm nervous because, for the past several weeks, inmates have been warning me about the judge presiding over my case. To make matters worse, Duana agrees when I ask her if what they've been saying is true.

"They call him Hanging Hancock," inmates tell me.

"Why?" I ask.

"He's real mean."

"He gave his own son ten years for selling drugs."

"I feel sorry for you."

"You better pray for another judge."

"What does he look like?" I ask. "Is he one of those undercover nigger-hating white racists?"

"No. He's black. Black, old, mean, and gray."

"I'm going to see if I can get you another judge," Duana tells me.

I spend the last few weeks praying that this mean old judge is too sick to show up. But in case he does show up I create plan B: a letter begging Hanging Hancock to have mercy on my tender soul. I hand the letter to Duana the last time she pays me a visit.

"Please be sure to give this letter to my judge before sentencing."

"I will," Duana promised.

I'm excited because today I will finally know something. Not knowing is more nerve-racking than knowing, even if it is bad news.

"Let's go, Vanessa," yells the correctional officer.

"I'm coming," I shout back.

"Good luck," a half-sleeping Sandra tells me.

"Thanks." I scurry to the front of the pod and wait for the correctional officer to pop open the door.

"Where do you think you're going with those sneakers on?" the officer asks me. "You can't wear sneakers to court."

"Why not?"

"Because you might try to escape and with sneakers on you just might outrun us."

I scurry back to my cell and put on my worn-out brown plastic slippers. Then I'm let out of pod 300 to join the other nervous inmates scheduled for sentencing.

Amid the inmates lined up against a wall is Yo-Yo. I'm happy to see her. The big grin on her face tells me she's happy to see me, too. I squeeze into line right behind Yo-Yo and instantly sense she's anxious. I assume, just like many of us in that line, she's concerned about the amount of time she's facing for armed robbery and kidnapping.

"You have a bachelor's in biology. Why in the world would you rob a chicken joint and abduct the workers?" I say to Yo-Yo the very first time she tells me about her offense. "What's wrong with you?"

Yo-Yo giggles at my response and then gives me some lame reason for her actions. This isn't her first offense either. She's served time in Fulton County jail for selling drugs.

The correctional officer handcuffs each inmate, wrist to

wrist. We are led outside, loaded into a large white van, and driven to the courthouse. There we're uncuffed and thrown into a large holding cell with cinderblock walls and cold metal benches pinned to a concrete floor. We're told to wait until it's our turn to be judged.

I take a break from conversing with Yo-Yo and strike up a conversation with another inmate who has sorrow written all over her face. Like many inmates I've met, she doesn't look like a criminal. She looks to be in her early twenties, fairly attractive with eyes the color of a ripe hazelnut.

"What are you here for?" I ask.

"Murder."

"Murder? Oh my! Who did you kill?"

"My lover."

"You killed your boyfriend?"

"No, my girlfriend. I stabbed her to death. I'm charged with manslaughter."

"How much time are you facing?"

"Fifteen years in prison."

"Wow!"

"What about you?"

"The prosecution recommended five years: Three in prison and two on probation," I tell her. But I'm hoping they'll release me today."

"I wish I was only facing five years."

Sadness for her comes over me as she tells me all about the incident with her dead girlfriend. She seems like such a sweet girl. She also tells me she has a young son. I feel sorry for him, too. He'll be a grown man by the time she's released.

After sitting in that holding cell for a couple of hours, mine, Yo-Yo's, and a couple other inmates' names are finally called. We are cuffed and escorted to different courtrooms.

On the right and left sides of the courtroom are pew-style wooden benches. There are tables at the front of the wooden benches, on both sides. Water pitchers and plastic cups sit on the tables. At the front of the courtroom is a raised desk, but no judge is sitting there. Adjacent to the raised desk is an empty witness stand and nearby, at a smaller desk, sits a court reporter.

A bailiff escorts me to the pew on the right side and then he stands against the wall. Soon after, spectators and parties or witnesses to the cases to be presented that day enter the courtroom. I see Angela Spivey, a friend of mine, walk into the courtroom and take a seat on the benches on the left side. She sees me and waves. I smile and wave back.

"Who is that?" the nosy bailiff asks me.

"My sister," I lie, thinking only family members are allowed inside the courtroom.

"She's pretty," the bailiff tells me. "I'll be right back. I want to talk to your sister."

While the bailiff talks to Angie, I spot the so called victim as she enters the courtroom. She's with one of Lucifer's associates. She sees me too and rolls her eyes. I roll mine right back at her. She walks over to the benches on the right side, a few rows behind me. After a few minutes I feel someone breathing down my neck. I turn around to find out it's the so called victim. Oooh! I so want to deck her. Instead I simply look her and her flunky dead in the eyes. After giving her one of those you-better-not-try-anything looks, I roll my eyes at both of them. Then I turn back around to face the front of the courtroom, hoping that the bailiff hurries up and gets back before this Gormless-Drama-Queen-Twit thinks about doing something stupid, like punching me in the back of my head.

He finally makes his way back over to my side of the room and posts himself back up against the wall.

"I thought you said Angie is your sister?" he asks me.

"She is. She's my spiritual sister." I change the subject. "So where's the judge?"

At last! A black man wearing a black robe walks through a door behind the raised desk. Until I see the name Michael E. Hancock inscribed on the name plate on the desk, I'm not quite sure if he's Hanging Hancock. Except for the fact that he's black, he looks nothing like how the inmates described him. I see a black man who looks to be in his fifties. I search for the gray hairs and don't see any. I try to find a mean streak on his face. None. He sits behind the desk and calls a few cases before mine.

"Is she the one who did the stabbing?" I overhear Hanging Hancock ask the assistant prosecuting attorney, a petite black woman. He looks in my direction and I detect a look of surprise on his face when the assistant prosecutor tells him, "Yes, that's her." The surprised look, I assume, is because I look nothing like a Gormless-Drama-Queen-Twit, the role I played eight months ago on that balmy summer evening.

He calls my name. The nosy bailiff escorts me to the front of the courtroom, then steps aside. Sitting on the left side of the courtroom in the front pew is Duana. I quickly walk to her and she tells me to sit beside her. She offers me some water. I decline.

"Did you give him my letter?" I whisper.

"Yes," Duana says, then goes on to tell me she had no luck getting a different judge. Duh! I'm not surprised. But I'm glad Duana failed. I feel good about Hancock. I sense that he has a soft spot for me. Duana asks me if I'm sure I don't want to take this case to trial.

"Will I get more than five years if I lose?" I've been hearing inmates say losing at a trial means double the original time that was recommended by the prosecution.

"Perhaps," Duana says.

"I think I'll stick with the guilty plea." I'm not going to risk five years for ten or more. Besides, Duana did not have enough ammunition to get my bail reduced; nor did she have enough to get my felony reduced to a misdemeanor; nor was she able to get a different judge to preside over my case. So why in the world would I expect this inexperienced, though very sweet, woman to have enough ammo to win my case at a trial? I need money and a real lawyer if I want to fight this case at a trial and/or the Almighty Power, whose laws I have not been abiding by. Therefore, He may not be willing to help a sister out of this jam. But I still pray for His favor.

Half an hour later my case is over and done. I'm not at all surprised that the so called victim stood in front of the judge and gave him attitude and lies while giving her version of what happened on the day in question.

"Look what she did to me!" the so called victim cried out. "All we were doing was arguing and she went overboard."

"How much time do you think she should spend in jail?" Hancock asks her.

"Forever!"

"Why? She doesn't strike me as a violent person."

"Because I have to wear this scar forever!"

I could tell by the look on Hancock's face he was hardly buying her lies. Her newest adaptation didn't quite match up with the hard copy script. And based on her courtroom performance, it was pretty clear who the true troublemaker in this case was. Unfortunately for me, you can't bring a knife to a fist fight. You automatically become the accused, even if the other person is the real perpetrator.

I am convicted of aggravated assault. And as I had hoped, I did not hear, "Time served! You're free to go home, young lady." Instead I hear, "Here's what I'm going to do. I am going to sentence you to two years in prison and three years probation."

"Does she get credit for the time served?" Duana asks.

"Yes. She'll get credit for the time she has served."

I'm a tad disappointed I have to remain behind bars for another sixteen months; however, I am relieved and thankful I do not have to serve the three years in prison recommended by the prosecution. Whew! Hanging Hancock did, after all, have a tiny soft spot in his heart for me. I don't care what *they* say. In my book, he's no Hanging Hancock. He's Compassionate Hancock.

Back in cuffs again, I'm led out of the courtroom back to the holding cell where I anxiously await the verdicts of some of the other inmates who rode in the van with me. I'm especially anxious to know the amount of time Yo-Yo has to serve, if any. I wait about an hour before the other inmates return to the holding cell. Yo-Yo and the other young woman, the one with the hazelnut eyes, aren't as fortunate as I am. Yo-Yo is sentenced to ten years and must serve six of them in prison. Hazelnut eyes is sentenced to twenty-something years and must serve fifteen in prison.

Chapter Twenty-Seven

May 22, 2000.

"Vanessa Murray, pack it up!" yells the on-duty officer from the control booth. I jump out of bed and notice it's one-thirty in the wee hours.

It's been nearly seven weeks to the day I was sentence. I don't have to ask what's going on. Everybody knows that when an officer yell "Pack it up!" you're either going home or to prison. I still have less than fifteen months to serve, so I know I'm not going home.

A few hours earlier I'd celebrated my thirty-eighth birthday in a quiet corner of my cell, where the chocolate cupcake I bought from the commissary was my make-believe birthday cake. "Happy birthday to me," I quietly sang before making a wish and shoving the cake down my throat.

"Hurry up, Murray!"

"I'm coming!" I turn to Sandra, who's now awake. "If she

keeps that up, she's going to wake the dead." I throw my books, pictures, and love letters from Yo-Yo in my commissary bag. Then I hug a teary-eyed Sandra before leaving my cell.

"I'm'ma miss you, Vanessa," Sandra calls out as I walk to the front of the pod. "You better write me and let me know what prison they stick you in."

"Okay, I will."

The squad car ride to Metro State Prison in Atlanta takes no more than fifteen minutes. The police officer opens the back door and helps me and another inmate out, removes the cuffs from our wrists, and leaves us with two female correctional officers. As we walk toward the barbed wire facility I spot Yo-Yo, who was shipped here five days ago, sporting a white jumpsuit and black combat boots. She's marching with a bunch of other inmates in the same getup. "Yo' left, yo' left, yo' left, right, left," they chant.

"What is this, the army?" I whisper to the inmate that rode with me.

"I know. Right. What the hell is this?" she whispers back. We giggle.

"You think this is funny?!" one of the officers yells, looking in my direction.

"No," I say, looking sheepish.

She moves in close to me. "When I ask you a question, inmate, your response should be 'Ma'am, no, ma'am' or 'Ma'am, yes, ma'am.' Is that understood, inmate?"

"Yes, sir. I mean, yes, ma'am." I look at the other inmate and see her struggle to conceal a smirk, which nearly causes me to burst out laughing in the officer's face.

"I see you don't follow directions very well, inmate." She moves in closer, our noses nearly touching. I feel her hot breath on my face. "Are you eyeballing me, inmate?"

"No."

"No what?" she screams. "Did we already forget how to address an officer?"

"No, ma'am."

"Do you not understand English or are you a retard? I told you to start your sentence with ma'am and end it with ma'am!"

"Ma'am, no, ma'am." Whew!

We finally reach inside the prison grounds. The guard commands us to join a few other new arrivals standing in line and escorts us into a building where more officers await.

"If you got braids, twists, or locks in your hair, take 'em out now!" shouts an officer. "And make it quick, before I cut your hair off."

"I just got my hair freshly done up yesterday," I say to one of the other arrivals.

The front half of my hair is in tiny cornrows going back. The back part is twisted in two strands. I look sort of cute with my fresh new do, if I must say so myself. But with the help of another new arrival, I take my hair apart. Now I look like a hot mess.

"Take off your clothes!" shouts a female prison guard.

"Everything?" I ask.

"Yes, take it all off, inmate. And put it in here."

The guard hands me a black garbage bag. I put in my orange county-jail suit, panties, and bra and set the bag aside. Whatever dignity I have left is stripped off with my clothes. I cross my arms over my small breasts to cover some of the humiliation. Then the guard tells me to squat and cough. I do it, while she looks up my butthole and down my throat with a flashlight. Then she hoses me down with a sticky fluid that smells like roach spray. She sprays it in my hair and on my coochie. "Lift up your arms. Straight up, like this." She sprays the sticky stuff onto my armpits. I try hard to hold back the tears welling up in my eyes as she hands me a small bar of soap and instructs me to stand in a shower stall with no door. "Wash your hair. And hurry up! You only get two minutes." Two minutes is hardly enough time to properly wash and rinse away that sticky stuff, but I do the best I can under the circumstances. Then I dry off with the towel the guard hands me. "Here! Put these on."

From her hand I grab a white jumpsuit, pair of panties, and bra. Appalled, I shove them back at her—the panties and bra—thinking she must've fallen and bumped her head this morning.

"I am not putting these on!" I shout. "Do you see what you gave me? These are dirty, and not even my size."

"Yes, you are!" the guard shouts back.

"No, I'm not! These panties have piss stains on them and the bra is dingy. That's unsanitary. I'm not putting this on."

"Yes, you are!"

"No, I'm not! Can I just put back on the panty and bra I wore here?"

"No! Put on what I gave you."

Lucky for me the guard turns her back to address another matter. I swiftly grab the black bag, throw in the corroded undergarments, grab and put on my clean ones, and slide into the white jumpsuit, seconds before the guard turns back to me. She gives me a pair of black combat boots and, while my hair is still wet and messy, instructs me to sit in front of a camera as another prison guard snaps photographs.

Prison mug shot of Vanessa taken at Metro State Prison

Chapter Twenty-Eight

Diagnostic precedes permanent placement at one of the four women's prison in Georgia. All new arrivals get medical examinations and psychological tests, then thorough instruction in the rules and regulations of the prison world. We learn how to properly address an employee, which I learned earlier. We learn how to march. "Attention...about face...forward march...at ease!" We learn military-style songs. Most of them are made up by inmates. "Yo' left, yo' left, yo' left, right, left...I used to wear my Tommy Hills, but now they got me doing drills...."

My day starts at the crack of dawn, beginning with count time. This is to make sure no one has escaped since the last count. Count time takes place several times throughout the day.

After the first count, I quickly change into my white jumpsuit, head outside in a single file line, and sing and march all the way to the dining hall, where breakfast is served. After breakfast we march back to the dorm and clean it from top to bottom. I have never been in the armed forces, but I imagine that this is what it must be like, minus the ugly white jumpsuit and the degrading portion, which by the way I am growing accustomed to. Cleaning entails dusting, mopping, waxing, buffing, making my bed tight and neat, and folding the tip of a roll of toilet paper a certain way. *How ridiculous*, I think. After we spend all morning cleaning, we get a visit from the inspection team. If dust is found on one of the inspectors' white gloves, an infraction is given to the inmate or inmates whose room is improperly cleaned. After inspection is approved and cleared, we march and sing some more. We march to the medical building or testing sites or we just march around in circles to pass the time away.

Oh, how I wish I was serving the rest of my time at Dekalb County Jail. At least there I didn't have to march around all day. I didn't have to do anything but sleep my time away, if that's what I chose to do.

Classification is the final phase of diagnostic. It takes place immediately after all the examinations have been conducted.

Inmates are assigned to a security level between one and five. Level one is trusty security. At this level inmates have proven trustworthy and cooperative and are therefore allowed to work for limited amounts of time without immediate supervision. The next levels are minimum (two), medium (three), close (four), and maximum (five).

Because of the nature of my crime I'm assigned the highest level, five. Inmates at this level are considered dangerous and violent, requiring supervision at all times.

One white woman sits on death row. Kelly Gissendaner. She's the only female inmate on death row in the state of Georgia. I wonder what category or level death row falls under. I guess it's level five, since that's the highest. She's kept in solitary caging all day, although I did see her on the grounds once, shackled and escorted by members of the Community Emergency Response Team. All movement stopped until she passed by.

I hear she's a former prison guard and mother of three. I hear she was convicted of scheming with her boyfriend to kidnap and murder her husband in order to get possession of a house and $20,000 in insurance money. I don't know if this is true, but it's what I hear from other inmates and news articles. Her boyfriend got a life sentence with the likelihood of parole in exchange for testifying against her.

From time to time I run into Jeannette on the prison grounds. She's been here since February. She's already been through Diagnostic and Classification. She's now part of the general prison population and wears a two-piece beige outfit. She tells me she has less than two weeks before she'll be set free. She gives me an address where I can reach her and tells me to write her. "I will," I promise. Then, in case I don't run into her again before she sets foot in the free world, I wish her all the best in her endeavors.

I see Yo-Yo more regularly. Although she's not housed in my dorm, she's still going through Diagnostic and Classification, too, which means we usually end up marching to the same places and doing the same things daily. We even sit and chat together in the park during recreation time.

Chapter Twenty-Nine

"Murray, pack it up!" yells the on-duty prison guard. I jump out of bed and gather my belongings. For a quick second in my sleepy state I think I'm going home. But then I remember I still have thirteen more months to serve. My time in the diagnostic facility is over and I'm ready to be permanently placed—whether here at Metro State Prison or at another institution, remains to be seen. I don't know why, but I pray it's not here.

I'm happy to see Yo-Yo waiting in the holding area. This could only mean one thing: she too is on the schedule to join general population.

We both find out we're going to another institution. Then when Yo-Yo, a couple of other inmates, and I are shackled together, ankle to ankle like girls in a chain gang, we realize we're all going to the same prison.

The long ride there is a welcome break after three grueling weeks of diagnostic. In the big white van we all have a friendly conversation and a few laughs and jokes. I even get cozy enough to slide off my cuffs.

"Girl, you better put those cuffs back on," Yo-Yo whispers. "They might charge you with trying to escape if they see your cuffs off."

After I slide my cuffs back on, I take Yo-Yo up on her other suggestion and lay my head on her chest and catnap for the remainder of the ride, a ride that lasts over two hours.

Pulaski State Prison is located in Hawkinsville, Georgia. It is a maximum-security facility. It's huge, sort of like a college campus except for the barbed wire fences. As an officer leads us onto the prison grounds and into the check-in building, I see inmates dressed in sky blue and white uniforms going to and fro, unsupervised. I have no idea where they're going but I'm sure I'll be joining them soon.

I spot Sierra, the crackhead I befriended at Dekalb County Jail. I call out her name and she turns and gives me a wave and a smile. She looks well. Her skin is clear; her hair is fuller and longer. I must say, prison has done wonders for her. She looks absolutely stunning and healthy, nothing like she looked at the county jail.

After check-in Yo-Yo and I, with all the other new arrivals, are dumped in building E9, a huge dorm with nearly two hundred other inmates doubled up in tiny cells. My cellmate is a white chick serving time for embezzling funds from her former job. She's cool, quiet, clean, and minds her own business. Just like me, she doesn't want any drama, I can tell. That's my kind of cellmate.

It's extremely crowded and noisy up in this dorm. But as with any situation that's thrust upon me, I quickly learn to adapt to my new life as a piece of property of the state of Georgia.

My daily work detail is the night orderly. My job entails cleaning shower stalls, mopping, waxing, and buffing the huge dorm floor, all for no pay.

Here the warden seems more concerned with making sure all the floors look shiny and new than she is with anything else.

A few of the inmates go behind my back and tell the counselor assigned to my dorm that I'm not doing a good job cleaning the shower stalls. The counselor threatens to assign me to the kitchen. Then she looks at my face for any signs of concern. I don't respond to her silly threat, nor do I show her any emotions, so she changes the subject. Maybe she takes into consideration that, number one, the look on my face says, "I don't care if I work in that gnat infested kitchen," and number two, putting me on a detail that requires the use of knives might be a bad idea.

Yo-Yo is seeing another woman now.

"You dumped me for that?" I jokingly say. "She looks like the back of my shoe."

Yo-Yo and I roar with laughter, then Yo-Yo tries to explain that she's only with the shoe-face woman because she buys Yo-Yo lots of things.

No need to explain. Yo-Yo and I have become more like friends than lovers. Besides women ain't really my thing. I was just having a moment. I'm strictly dickly, as *they* say. And if I wasn't, my inner voice keeps reminding me that I'd better be if I don't want the wrath of my Maker to come upon me for disobeying one of His commandments: *Thou shalt not lie with womankind, as with mankind: it is an abomination.*

I now understand how easy it is to fall into that kind of lifestyle when incarcerated for a long time. Bull-dagging, as we call it in here, sort of goes along with the territory.

It isn't long before Yo-Yo is seen in the arms of *another* woman.

"Much better," I tell Yo-Yo.

"I'm glad you approve of this one."

"Yeah, she's pretty. She doesn't look like the back of my shoe."

Chapter Thirty

As I near the end of my prison sentence my security level drops down to minimum, making me eligible for work release.

In November 2000 I'm transported back to Atlanta to serve the remainder of my time at Metro Transitional Center, a half-way house. The center is right next door to Metro State Prison and about five miles away from my sister's apartment, give or take. She visits often.

I don't immediately adapt to my new abode and new set of laws. They overwhelm me until I actually sob like a baby my very first day. The next day isn't much better, except for the moment I'm cheered by the sight of Sierra. She looks even better than the last time I saw her, now that she's in civilian clothes.

"How long have you been here?" I ask.

"About four months now," Sierra says. "I have a good job

making eleven dollars an hour."

Because Sierra is one of the working residents, her living quarters are on the opposite side of the facility from nonworking residents, like me. So I see little of her. But whenever I do see her, she slips me five dollars so I can buy snacks and stuff from the vending machines. What a sweetie pie she is.

Two weeks go by and I'm still not adjusting to this place very well. Standing on my feet every time a correctional officer comes into view annoys me deeply. What a dumb rule, especially since they come into view at least every five minutes. No talking. Another dumb rule. Do they really expect the residents never to talk in here? Dumb!

I can't become a working resident until after I successfully complete a six-week orientation phase, during which time residents must wear a two-piece beige prison uniform, attend workshops a couple of times a week, and clean the whole center, sometimes with a toothbrush. If there are no workshops to attend, cleaning is done from sunup to sundown, even though there's nothing left to clean. Dumb! Just plain ol' dumb!

When I finally obtain a full-time second-shift job, it requires me to stand on my feet all night. Standing doesn't work out for me, considering the long bus ride to the job site makes me sick. Motion sickness is a problem I've had to battle since childhood. I spend half of my time at work running to the restroom either to throw up or to sit down on the toilet before I pass out. By the time I arrive back at the half-way center, well past midnight, I'm dizzy and nauseated from the long bus ride back. I can't lie down straightaway because first I have to take a breathalyzer test and then strip, squat, and cough. I can't take this dehumanizing treatment much longer. Stripping is the main rule I can't seem to adapt to. I'm fed up with these folk looking in my butthole each day. "I don't have anything in it but dooky," I tell one of the staff members. "I wanna go back to prison and finish my time there. I'm sick of this."

February 2001.

After roughly three months at the transitional center I'm expelled for insubordination, so *they* claim. All I did was give one of the correctional officers a piece of my mind with one simple word: snitch. And then *bam*! I'm slapped with a disciplinary report and discharged. The news that I must leave the facility is bittersweet. Bitter because I will no longer be halfway free, allowed to do such things as wear civilian clothes, eat real food, and sneak to the Perimeter Mall. Sweet because there'll be no more booty inspections and motion sicknesses.

"Be careful what you ask for," as *they* say. "It just might come true."

I'm transported back to Pulaski State Prison to finish the

five remaining months of my time. But first I have to spend a week housed in the segregation/isolation building (a jail inside prison for defiant inmates) at Metro State Prison.

Chapter Thirty One

July 31, 2001.

"Murray, pack it up!" yells a correctional officer.

She doesn't have to tell me twice. As a matter of fact, she didn't have to tell me once. I've been packed and ready to go since last night. I haven't even slept because I'm too keyed up. I've spent the last two years waiting for this moment. Do they really think I'm going to allow packing to slow me down from getting out of this beast? I bang on my cell door. "Pop open my door! I'm ready already."

On the way to the check-out building—where a twenty-five dollar check, release paper, bus ticket to Atlanta, cheesy pink two-piece outfit, and cheesy pink shoes await me—I spot Yo-Yo standing in front of the medical facility.

"Bye, Yo-Yo," I call out. "I'm gon'na miss you."

"Bye, Vanessa. Write me."

"Okay, I might."

"And don't go back to that fat man!" We both laugh.

"Don't worry, I won't."

Part V

Truth is Torah

Chapter Thirty-Two

In the beginning was Torah and Torah was with YHWH and Torah was YHWH. By way of Torah YHWH created ALL things, including the Heavens and Earth and all that therein is.

Torah is simply the instructions in righteousness, the law and commandments given by YHWH to His creation for its own good and well-being. And the same law and commandments that brought ALL into existence are the same ones to sustain it. Therefore, Torah is the way, Torah is Truth, and Torah is life. So, contrary to popular belief, Torah has not been abolished or done away with. In fact, obedience to Torah, and the fear of YHWH, is the whole duty of man. Roger that!

Epilogue

My mysterious son survived the bullets sprayed at him during the alleged drug-related incident that landed him in Harlem Hospital, a bullet lodged in his thigh yet to be removed. The shooter was never found, at least not by the cops.

My son also survived a knife that was plunged into his lower back during a fight with rival gang members. Many more predicaments followed, but somehow my son's life was miraculously spared while some of his codefendants weren't.

Is his life being preserved for a specific purpose, I often ponder. *Is that the reason why I somehow was unable to abort him?*

It seemed as if he was getting away with too many things that most wouldn't escape, that most didn't escape.

"Wow! That's got to be the Most High protecting you," I'd say to my son time and time again. "You better catch a clue and stop doing whatever it is you're doing before God's mercy depart away from you."

What is to become of my son remains to be seen. In the meantime he's no longer participating in gang activities and he's made me a grandmother, and his sister an aunt, to the cutest little girl who's the mirror image of him. I call her Tootie.

After Jeannette was released I wrote to the address she gave me but never received a response. I later found out that she'd been arrested again for violating her nine-year probation, and a new charge was added.

About a week after I was kicked out of the halfway house, Sierra went AWOL. She was arrested a few days later at a crack house on Candler Road in Decatur, Georgia.

In 2006 the so called victim died when she fell, sustaining injuries to her brain. My sincere condolences go out to her children.

As for me, after my release, I didn't wallow in self-pity over the wrong choices I made. Instead, I picked myself up, dusted the dirt off my shoulders, and kept it moving onto the next chapter of my life. In the next chapter I dabbled into property buying, returned to school, and most importantly, Truth stepped into my life and set me free from some of the greatest lies and fairy tales many of us inherited when we were born.

Food-for-thought: If they don't treat you right, they won't teach you right!

LaVergne, TN USA
24 November 2010
206097LV00001B/13/P

9 781936 400737